BRITISH AUTHORS

Introductory Critical Studies

GEORGE ELIOT

In this series

John Keats by ROBIN MAYHEAD
William Wordsworth by GEOFFREY DURRANT
Jane Austen by YASMINE GOONERATNE

GEORGE ELIOT

BY

R. T. JONES

Senior Lecturer in English
University of York

CAMBRIDGE
AT THE UNIVERSITY PRESS
1970

Published by the Syndics of the Cambridge University Press
Bentley House, 200 Euston Road, London N.W.1
American Branch: 32 East 57th Street, New York, N.Y. 10022

© Cambridge University Press 1970

Library of Congress Catalogue Card Number: 75-114602

Standard Book Numbers:
521 07832 6 clothbound
521 09613 8 paperback

Printed in Great Britain
at the University Printing House, Cambridge
(Brooke Crutchley, University Printer)

GENERAL PREFACE

This study of George Eliot is the fourth in a series of short introductory critical studies of the more important British authors. The aim of the series is to go straight to the authors' works; to discuss them directly with a maximum of attention to concrete detail; to say what they are and what they do, and to indicate a valuation. The general critical attitude implied in the series is set out at some length in my *Understanding Literature*. Great literature is taken to be to a large extent self-explanatory to the reader who will attend carefully enough to what it says. 'Background' study, whether biographical or historical, is not the concern of the series.

It is hoped that this approach will suit a number of kinds of reader, in particular the general reader who would like an introduction which talks about the works themselves; and the student who would like a general critical study as a starting point, intending to go on to read more specialized works later. Since 'background' is not erected as an insuperable obstacle, readers in other English-speaking countries, countries where English is a second language, or even those for whom English is a foreign language, should find the books helpful. In Britain and the Commonwealth, students and teachers in universities and in the higher forms of secondary schools will find that the authors chosen for treatment are those most often prescribed for study in public and university examinations.

The series could be described as an attempt to make available to a wide public the results of the literary criticism of the last thirty years, and especially the methods associated with Cambridge. If the result is an increase in the reading, with enjoyment and understanding, of the great works of English literature, the books will have fulfilled their wider purpose.

ROBIN MAYHEAD

CONTENTS

1 Introductory   *page* 1

2 *Adam Bede*   6

3 *The Mill on the Floss*   19

4 *Silas Marner*   31

5 *Felix Holt*   43

6 *Middlemarch*   57

7 *Daniel Deronda*   97

Note. The page numbers that follow quotations
from the novels refer to the *Everyman* editions

1

INTRODUCTORY

I am sorry that our good friend Forman has republished his criticisms, because I think there is more than enough literature of the criticising sort urged upon people's attention by the periodicals. To read much of it seems to me seriously injurious: it accustoms men and women to formulate opinions instead of receiving deep impressions, and to receive deep impressions is the foundation of all true mental power.

(The George Eliot Letters, ed. G. S. Haight, v, 155)

George Eliot was surely right, and this book is written with a sense of the impertinence of adding yet another volume on her work to the large bulk of 'literature of the criticizing sort' that already exists. This addition can be justified only if, by drawing attention to some aspects of George Eliot's novels that might have been overlooked, it can help the reader to receive for himself the 'deep impressions' that the novels can make. One can only hope that it will not result in substituting second-hand opinions for the felt impact of the novels themselves.

George Eliot was not only a novelist. She was also a brilliant essayist, and deserves to be studied as such. One of the difficulties of writing about her novels is that she herself formulated and explored, in her essays, most of the central concerns of her novels, with a strenuous precision that we can hardly hope to equal. Here, for example, in a paragraph from Chapter XIII of *Impressions of Theophrastus Such* (a series of essays), George Eliot discusses matters of central relevance to her novels, and most directly to her use of such phrases as 'Have we not all...' and 'Which of us has not...':

Introspection which starts with the purpose of finding out one's own absurdities is not likely to be very mischievous, yet of course it is not free from dangers any more than breathing is, or the other functions that keep us alive and active. To judge of others by oneself is in its most innocent meaning the briefest expression for our only method of knowing mankind; yet, we perceive, it has come to mean in many cases either the vulgar mistake which reduces every man's value to the very low figure at which the valuer himself happens to stand; or else, the amiable illusion of the higher nature misled by a too generous construction of the lower. One cannot give a recipe for wise judgment: it resembles appropriate muscular action, which is attained by the myriad lessons in nicety of balance and of aim that only practice can give. The danger of the inverse procedure, judging of self by what one observes in others, if it is carried on with much impartiality and keenness of discernment, is that it has a laming effect, enfeebling the energies of indignation and scorn, which are the proper scourges of wrong-doing and meanness, and which should continually feed the wholesome restraining power of public opinion. I respect the horsewhip when applied to the back of Cruelty, and think that he who applies it is a more perfect human being because his outleap of indignation is not checked by a too curious reflection on the nature of guilt—a more perfect human being because he more completely incorporates the best social life of the race, which can never be constituted by ideas that nullify action. This is the essence of Dante's sentiment (it is painful to think that he applies it very cruelly)—

'E cortesia fù, lui esser villano'—

and it is undeniable that a too intense consciousness of one's kinship with all frailties and vices undermines the active heroism which battles against wrong.

This prose is as tightly packed as almost any that we could find in the novels. Its generalizations about humanity have the authority of long and systematic observation. The clear recognition of the dangers of introspection as a method (although it is our only method) of understanding other people marks a mind that habitually studies, checks and evaluates its own modes of activity. 'One cannot give a recipe for wise judgment' is a forceful, direct and homely expression of a highly complex sense of what moral judgment means, and this is followed by an analogy that is almost a poetic image (drawn, as George Eliot's images often are, from the physical sciences): 'it resembles appropriate muscular action, which is attained by the myriad lessons in nicety of balance and of aim that only practice can give'. The comparison suggests that judging wisely is an almost inconceivably complex process, just as the activity of walking involves numerous nerves and muscles of which we are hardly aware, registering and correcting our incipient imbalances at every step, making countless small adjustments of force and tension in response to the changing nature of the ground and even to the strength and direction of the wind, as well as to our decisions about the way we choose to walk. It is possible that

George Eliot was led to these considerations by thinking about the biblical image of 'walking in the paths of righteousness'; it is certain that she has enriched it.

The second half of the paragraph describes, more lucidly than any critic's account, the danger to which George Eliot's fiction is most exposed: that of extending sympathy so generously to all human weakness that it might 'enfeeble the energies of indignation and scorn', and thus 'undermine the active heroism which battles against wrong'. By being so clearly aware of this danger, she is able to avoid it; if we, her readers, are to avoid it, we need to be aware of it too. If, partly as a consequence of George Eliot's fiction, tolerance is more highly valued as a social virtue now than it was in her time, we are correspondingly more vulnerable to the enfeeblement and the undermining that she describes.

This book will not concern itself with George Eliot's essays, nor with her tales and poems. It will, I hope, be clear by now that this does not imply a low valuation of the essays, but a very high one of the novels. (I omit the poems because, at their best, they are flawed fiction—flawed because metre was hardly ever anything but an impediment to George Eliot's imagination; and the tales, though interesting, are left out for the sake of economy, because their merits are those of the novels in miniature.) One of my aims in the pages that follow will be to show how the art of George Eliot the novelist can reach further in understanding, in sympathetic imagination, and in the exploration of moral values, than can the expository and speculative prose of an essay—even when the essayist is George Eliot herself.

Impressions of Theophrastus Such is not a novel. It was the last book that George Eliot published, and she was concerned that it should be advertised in such a way as to make sure that people should not be misled into thinking that it was a novel. In fact, it begins almost as if it were one; but it soon becomes clear that the fictitious narrator is a vehicle for the author's own 'impressions' of various aspects of life. It exhibits the same impressive intellect, the same 'exemption from cerebral lassitude' (as Henry James calls it) that we find in the novels, but it is not creative in the same degree: it extends our understanding, but does not widen our experience. There are, indeed, imaginary characters in it, and their motives are relentlessly analysed; but they are representative types, examples to illustrate an argument, not created persons exhibiting a fully human range of actual and potential qualities.

Romola, on the other hand, is unquestionably a novel as far as its form is concerned, and George Eliot certainly regarded it as one. Its omission from the chapters that follow requires some explanation. It is set in Florence, in the fifteenth century, and is a remarkable achievement of historical research and historical imagination. In presenting the characters and their relationships, George Eliot undertakes a scholarly reconstruction of the texture of life in fifteenth-century Florence; and the language of the conversations is an attempt to represent in English the Italian of various classes of people in that city at that time. All this, most conscientiously done, left little freedom for the novelist's imagination, especially as several important historical personages play a large part in the story. A novelist speaks with authority, but a biographer must often speak conjecturally; when George Eliot portrays the monk Savonarola, or members of the Medici family, she can be a novelist only in the gaps between historical facts, and then only tentatively.

Perhaps it is because her sense of what is permanent in human nature was not free to direct her imagination, that it appears instead in the form of generalizing paragraphs and abstract accounts of motives and consequences. In *Romola*, the author's finest insights are expressed in the mode of the essayist, not the novelist. Thus it is in *Romola* that we find some of the most precise descriptions of processes that, in the other novels, we experience with the people involved in them. For example, when Tito Melema—in a scene that is spectacular rather than moving— has been suddenly confronted by his old benefactor, and has impulsively denied him, we are told that

he seemed to have spoken without any preconception: the words had leaped forth like a sudden birth that had been begotten and nourished in the darkness.

Tito was experiencing that inexorable law of human souls, that we prepare ourselves for sudden deeds by the reiterated choice of good and evil which gradually determines character. (Chapter XXIII)

4

This description of the origins of an unpremeditated action gives full recognition to the unconscious activities of the mind, and their power, under sudden stress, to exert a decisive and terrible influence over our actions; but it also suggests, both in the poetic image of the first sentence and in the more prosaic formulation of the second, how we can be held responsible for our unconsciously motivated actions. It is an illuminating and compelling account; we may well find it useful in describing events in the other novels (and, of course, events in our own lives); but our understanding of it is not enriched by any full imaginative participation in Tito's experience.

Romola ought, I think, to be read more often than it is. It contains, as I have suggested, a good deal of George Eliot's wisdom, which is worth having in any form, and some of the most concise and lucid formulations of those 'general laws' that she persistently sought in human behaviour and its consequences. But to discuss it at length beside such novels as, say, *Silas Marner* and *Middlemarch* would be, inevitably, to demonstrate more fully that it is something less than a novel. Even 'literature of the criticizing sort' can, I hope, find more useful work to do.

In discussing the other novels, in the order in which they were written, I shall comment on parts of each novel, in order to suggest the texture of thought and feeling, the quality of experience, offered by the whole. The difficulty is to decide which parts not to quote, which aspects of each novel not to represent; and it would be surprising if some readers should not consider my selections arbitrary. That does not matter; this is not an anthology, a selection of the finest passages. But I hope, in the course of the book, to draw attention to the central concerns of the novels, and to the principal critical problems that they raise.

2

'ADAM BEDE'

This is how the novel starts:

With a single drop of ink for a mirror, the Egyptian sorcerer undertakes to reveal to any chance comer far-reaching visions of the past. This is what I undertake to do for you, reader. With this drop of ink at the end of my pen, I will show you the roomy workshop of Mr. Jonathan Burge, carpenter and builder, in the village of Hayslope, as it appeared on the eighteenth of June, in the year of our Lord 1799. (7)

The novelist seems to be telling us that writing a novel, making real and present to us a past that is otherwise inaccessible, is a mysterious craft. George Eliot has served her apprenticeship in the craft of fiction by writing *Scenes of Clerical Life*, and can say 'I will show you' with confidence; but her confidence strikes us as an acknowledgement of the power of fiction rather than as expressing any arrogance about her own ability.

The paragraph that follows gives us more than a 'vision': it is a remarkably full communication of the experience of being in the workshop, involving scent and touch as well as sight.

The afternoon sun was warm on the five workmen there, busy upon doors and window-frames and wainscoting. A scent of pine-wood from a tent-like pile of planks outside the open door mingled itself with the scent of the elder-bushes which were spreading their summer snow close to the open window opposite; the slanting sunbeams shone through the transparent shavings that flew before the steady plane, and lit up the fine grain of the oak panelling which stood propped against the wall. On a heap of those soft shavings a rough grey shepherd-dog had made himself a pleasant bed, and was lying with his nose between his fore-paws, occasionally wrinkling his brows to cast a glance at the tallest of the five workmen, who was carving a shield in the centre of a wooden mantelpiece. (7)

Each element of this description is an achievement of remembered observation and sensuous response. The way in which a dog with its head at rest wrinkles its brows to look upwards, the transparency of flying wood shavings in sunlight, and the arrangement of planks stacked at the door of a carpenter's workshop—as well

6

as their scent—must have been appreciatively observed and carefully recalled. But the whole scene is fictitious; the synthesis of the impressions remembered from various times and places into the wholeness of a place, an environment, a texture of life, is a triumph not of recollection but of creative imagination.

This tangible reality of place is not to be regarded merely as a clever trick, by which the novelist adds a pleasant but momentary illusion of truth to a story of people who never existed. The value of the novel (and of her other novels) consists in its being, to use George Eliot's own phrase, *an experiment in life*—

an endeavour to see what our thought and emotion may be capable of—what stores of motive, actual or hinted as possible, give promise of a better after which we may strive—what gains from past revelations and discipline we must strive to keep hold of as something more sure than shifting theory.

(*The George Eliot Letters*, ed. G. S. Haight, VI, 216)

If fiction is to have the kind of validity implied by the scientific word 'experiment', as a means of discovering what really would happen in certain circumstances and not what one might wish to happen, the novelist's imagination must be at least as rigorously disciplined as the scientist's observation—more so, in fact, because the novelist's experiments are less accessible to objective verification. So George Eliot must first establish that the world in which the events of the novel take place really is the world we live in, governed by the same natural laws that govern human existence in the world we know. If she did not convince us of this, we could hardly take her findings seriously. And we recognize, in a novel, the real world we live in—as we recognize people and places we know—not so much by their measurable dimensions as by a whole range of miscellaneous impressions that we are often hardly aware of noticing.

The solid presence of a recognizably real world—that is the first requirement for a true fiction, and George Eliot supplies it throughout the novel. Sometimes, as in that description of the carpenter's workshop, she gives us the sense of it so abundantly that it affects us as an expression of delight in *things*, solid objects with shape and grain and texture. In the description of the dairy in which Hetty Sorrel makes butter, we have a symphony in colours and textures.

7

The dairy was certainly worth looking at: it was a scene to sicken for with a sort of calenture in hot and dusty streets—such coolness, such purity, such fresh fragrance of new-pressed cheese, of firm butter, of wooden vessels perpetually bathed in pure water; such soft colouring of red earthenware and creamy surfaces, brown wood and polished tin, grey limestone and rich orange-red rust on the iron weights and hooks and hinges. (82)

'Worth looking at'—but the imagination does not merely look: it picks up the objects and experiences their coolness, and their various kinds of solidity, their roughness or smoothness. The dairy is not merely a setting, a stage back-drop, for a scene in the novel: it is an environment that has a large part in determining the kinds of experience that can take place there. This is Hetty's world, as the carpenter's shop is Adam's; she is shown in a place to which she belongs, and the way in which we are led to look at her has been prepared by the description of the place. Again the visual impression is only a part of the whole presentation.

It is of little use for me to tell you that Hetty's cheek was like a rose-petal, that dimples played about her pouting lips, that her large dark eyes hid a soft roguishness under their long lashes, and that her curly hair, though all pushed back under her round cap while she was at work, stole back in dark delicate rings on her forehead, and about her white shell-like ears; it is of little use for me to say how lovely was the contour of her pink-and-white neckerchief, tucked into her low plum-coloured stuff bodice, or how the linen butter-making apron, with its bib, seemed a thing to be imitated in silk by duchesses, since it fell in such charming lines, or how her brown stockings and thick-soled buckled shoes lost all that clumsiness which they must certainly have had when empty of her foot and ankle;—of little use, unless you have seen a woman who affected you as Hetty affected her be-holders, for otherwise, though you might conjure up the image of a lovely woman, she would not in the least resemble that distracting kitten-like maiden...Hetty's was a spring-tide beauty; it was the beauty of young frisking things, round-limbed, gambolling, circumventing you by a false air of innocence—the innocence of a young star-browed calf, for example, that, being inclined for a promenade out of bounds, leads you a severe steeplechase over hedge and ditch, and only comes to a stand in the middle of a bog. (83)

Alerted to varieties of texture by the preceding description of the dairy, the reader responds to the imagined reality of Hetty with finger-tips as well as eyes. This response is discreetly reinforced by verbs implying the activity of Hetty's own fingers about her person—her hair is 'all pushed back' and her neckerchief 'tucked into' her bodice—and by the way in which her foot and ankle, though not visible, are made substantial. But it is significant that all this follows the introductory words 'It is of little use for me to tell you': for the novelist's point here is that no description of the tangible substance can convey an adequate impression of a person. Even a preliminary suggestion of the kind of person Hetty is requires some account of her character—a mere hint, but one that can be interpreted only by the active collaboration of the reader. 'Kitten-like maiden' and 'spring-tide beauty' are phrases that invite the reader to associate Hetty with impressions that would be very hard to define, but are nevertheless quite precise in their context.

One of the ways in which the novel gives a very clear impression of character is by giving examples of their ways of talking. Adam Bede's mother is revealed, in speeches like this one, as habitually inclined to foresee disaster.

'Nay, my lad, my lad, thee wouldstna go away an' break thy mother's heart, an' leave thy feyther to ruin. Thee wouldstna ha' 'em carry me to th' churchyard, an' thee not to follow me. I shanna rest i' my grave if I donna see thee at th' last; an' how's they to let thee know as I'm a-dyin', if thee't gone a-working' i' distant parts, an' Seth belike gone arter thee, and thy feyther not able to hold a pen for's hand shakin', besides not knowin' where thee art? Thee mun forgie thy feyther—thee munna be so bitter again' him. He was a good feyther to thee afore he took to th' drink. He's a clever workman, an' taught thee thy trade, remember, an's niver gen me a blow nor so much as an ill word—no, not even in's drink. Thee wouldstna ha'm go to the workhus—thy own feyther—an' him as was a fine-growed man an' handy at everythin' almost as thee art thysen, five-an'-twenty 'ear ago, when thee wast a baby at the breast.' (42)

It is not, I think, the imitation of the dialect, but the imaginative creation of the patterns of thought that gives us in this speech a sense of the quality of Lisbeth Bede's life, and of the world she inhabits. It is the world of the peasant, with little to distract the mind from the primal facts of birth, change and death; more precisely, the world of the peasant woman, for whom the tragic realities are more insistently present than for the man—who has his work as a link with a world outside. Not that Lisbeth is a tragic figure—her response to her world is too weak for that, consisting (as we know from her reported speech) largely of 'a sort of wail, the most irritating of all sounds where real sorrows are to be borne, and real work to be done'.

Mrs Poyser, on the other hand, is revealed by her speech as a woman accustomed and determined to dominate; she is the wife of a substantial farmer, and her insistence on gloomy prospects is not a reflection of a comfortless world but a rhetorical technique that she employs with fascinating skill to make others cry. Molly, the housemaid, has stumbled and spilt a quantity of beer; after Mrs Poyser's first outburst—

Poor Molly's tears were dropping fast by this time...while Mrs Poyser, opening the cupboard, turned a blighting eye upon her.

'Ah,' she went on, 'you'll do no good wi' crying an' making more wet to wipe up. It's all your own wilfulness, as I tell you, for there's nobody no call to break anything if they'll only go the right way to work. But wooden folks had need ha' wooden things t'handle. And here must I take the brown-and-white jug, as it's niver been used three times this year, and go down i' the cellar myself, and belike catch my death, and be laid up wi' inflammation'...

(220)

The gloomy consequences foreseen in this speech are not like those that fill Lisbeth Bede's talk, real sorrows and appropriate objects of anxiety; they are fantasies, introduced for the sake of their effects on the audience. However tender her heart may be ('If her tongue's keen her heart's tender', Adam says of her), there is a heartlessness, even a degree of cruelty, in her verbal treatment of those who have the misfortune to be under her authority, and there is obviously some self-deception in her belief that she scolds them for their own good. Yet the novel seems generally to invite us to see Mrs Poyser in a comic light, and the tears of her victims as amusingly inappropriate reactions—as though they were taking seriously something that ought to be enjoyed as a performance. Not that Mrs Poyser is anything but serious when she scolds—the rhetorical quality of the speech I have quoted shows how seriously she takes the task of scolding. The description of her house makes it clear that all she does must be done well, and she does her scolding as thoroughly as the rest of her domestic tasks.

By such means as these, George Eliot presents to us a world that we recognize as our own, and people whom we can accept as having enough imagined reality for the novel's purposes. In fact, the presentation itself—the process by which the novel leads us to imagine sympathetically the textures of other people's lives—*is* one of those purposes. In a chapter where she discusses some of her aims in the novel, George Eliot writes:

> In this world there are so many of these common coarse people, who have no picturesque sentimental wretchedness! It is so needful we should remember their existence, else we may happen to leave them quite out of our religion and philosophy, and frame lofty theories which only fit a world of extremes. Therefore let Art always remind us of them...There are few prophets in the world; few sublimely beautiful women; few heroes. I can't afford to give all my love and reverence to such rarities: I want a great deal of those feelings for my fellow-men, especially for the few in the foreground of the great multitude, whose faces I know, whose hands I touch, for whom I have to make way with kindly courtesy. (174)

Sympathy is one of the great moral positives in George Eliot's novels, and we must look more closely at her way of leading the reader into sympathetic understanding of people. Here, as an example, is Lisbeth Bede after her husband's death:

> Lisbeth had even mended a long-neglected and unnoticeable rent in the checkered bit of bed-curtain; for the moments were few and precious now in which she would be able to do the smallest office of respect or love for the still corpse, to which in all her thoughts she attributed some consciousness. Our dead are never dead to us until we have forgotten them: they can be injured by us, they can be wounded; they know all our penitence, all our aching sense that their place is empty, all the kisses we bestow on the smallest relic of their presence. And the aged peasant-woman most of all believes that her dead are conscious. (102)

The first sentence describes an action, a motive and a belief, noted, as it were, from outside; and, presented in this objective way, the attribution of consciousness to the corpse strikes us as a superstition remote from our own experience—it is an anthropologist's observation. The second sentence surprises us by being about *us*, and invites us to recognize in ourselves a tendency that is fundamentally the same as the one we had been observing, as if from a safe distance, in Lisbeth Bede. It may, in us, manifest itself in different actions, but we can no longer see Lisbeth as holding a superstitious belief that we are enlightened enough to call absurd. Our common humanity with her is established. But the fact remains that we are not just like her; she is a peasant woman and we are readers of George Eliot's novels. So the next sentence takes up the difference: the tendency to attribute some consciousness to the dead, which at first seemed to separate Lisbeth from us, then united her with us, at last differentiates her from us in degree—but the sympathy remains. George Eliot is careful to remind us that sympathetic understanding does not consist in a readiness to suppose that other people are just like us, or just as we should be if we were in their place; but an attempt to understand our own behaviour and to see it in a new light is often a necessary beginning of an attempt to understand other people.

Dinah Morris is a Methodist, and preaches; most readers are likely to be predisposed to regard early Methodism, open-air preaching, and preaching by women, as manifestations of a form of religious fanaticism inaccessible alike to reason and sympathy. George Eliot counters this prejudice in many ways throughout the novel; here is one instance:

As Dinah expressed it, 'she was never left to herself; but it was always given her when to keep silence and when to speak'. And do we not all agree to call rapid thought and noble impulse by the name of inspiration? After our subtlest analysis of the mental process, we must still say, as Dinah did, that our highest thoughts and our best deeds are all given to us. (112)

Again, the first sentence gives us an impression of the oddity of Dinah and her sect, with their belief that when they preached, or comforted the distressed, God spoke through their mouths. But the following sentences show that Dinah's experience is not different in kind from something that happens to most of us, even if we do not profess to believe in a Deity—and that even her way of talking about it is not so remote from ours as it looked at first. Again, George Eliot helps us to find a sympathetic understanding of the person who struck us at first as very different from ourselves, so different, perhaps, as to be incomprehensible, and therefore to arouse suspicion and hostility.

When Arthur's meeting with Hetty in the wood is described, the same appeal to our own experience is used to lead us to a fuller understanding of the relationship between the two.

Hetty lifted her long dewy lashes, and met the eyes that were bent towards her with a sweet, timid, beseeching look. What a space of time those three moments were, while their eyes met and his arms touched her! Love is such a simple thing when we have only one-and-twenty summers and a sweet girl of seventeen trembles under our glance, as if she were a bud first opening her heart with wondering rapture to the morning. (129)

Afterwards, in the Hermitage, Arthur

first walked four or five times up and down the scanty length of the little room, and then seated himself on the ottoman in an uncomfortable stiff way, as we often do when we wish not to abandon ourselves to feeling. (130)

Thus, many times in the novel, George Eliot uses some such phrase as 'Have we not all...?' or 'Which of us has not...?' to enforce our imaginative participation in the feelings and actions of others. Even when no such phrase is used, the same appeal is usually implicit in the novelist's descriptions of the various ways in which people think and feel: her basic assumption is that no human act or emotion is entirely unconnected with what we have all done or felt at some time.

It is this firm belief in a common humanity, a certain range of feelings actually or potentially available to us all, so that however individuals may differ superficially it is never impossible for them to understand each other and to recognize their likeness to each other, that enables George Eliot to see her novels as contributing to establish general truths about humanity. By continually inviting the reader to look into his own heart for a better understanding of others, she not only cultivates in us a habit of sympathy, but also makes us aware of forces that operate in the lives of people in general—aware of

the presence of undeviating law in the material and moral world—of that invariability of sequence which is acknowledged to be the basis of physical science, but which is still perversely ignored in our social organization, our ethics and our religion.

These words come from her review, in 1851, of R. W. Mackay's *The Progress of the Intellect*. Eight years later, as a novelist, her conviction of the inevitability of consequences is as strong as before, but she formulates it differently. Adam Bede says,

'...I've seen pretty clear, ever since I could cast up a sum, as you can never do what's wrong without breeding sin and trouble more than you can ever see...'

13

Adam's implied analogy, between the moral consequences of a wrong action and the logical sequence of an arithmetical calculation, goes with his conviction that moral problems have correct solutions, like problems in arithmetic. In this respect his formulation is rather like George Eliot's earlier use of an implied analogy between ethics and physical science. But in the novel, Adam's confidence, which seems to derive from his mastery of his craft and to be expressed in his habitual phrase 'I've seen pretty clear', is to be profoundly shaken by the moral complexity of events in which he is later involved; and the unsure basis of his certainty is hinted at in the words he uses here. The analogy shifts from 'casting up a sum' to the more uncertain, and even mysterious, 'breeding sin and trouble'; and by the end of the sentence it turns out that what he 'sees pretty clear' is that you *can't* see the consequences of wrong-doing. Adam in his old age still uses the phrase 'I've seen pretty clear'; but his view of the inevitable sequence of cause and effect seems to have been modified by his experience:

'... I know there's a deal in a man's inward life as you can't measure by the square, and say, "Do this and that'll follow", and "Do that and this'll follow."' (177)

But the novel shows that in the outward life too, consequences acquire an unpredictable momentum of their own, and grow utterly disproportionate to the act that started them.

The twists and turns of decision and indecision that lead up to Arthur's making love to Hetty are presented in a series of detailed analyses of his thoughts. Here I can only suggest the depth and subtlety of the portrayal with a few brief illustrations. Just before his second meeting with Hetty in the wood, we are told:

He is going to see Hetty again: that is the longing which has been growing through the last three hours to a feverish thirst. Not, of course, to speak in the caressing way into which he had unguardedly fallen before dinner, but to set things right with her by a kindness which would have the air of friendly civility, and prevent her from running away with wrong notions about their mutual relation. (133)

In the description of the dairy where we first saw Hetty—it is quoted on page 8—we were told that it was 'a scene to sicken for with a sort of calenture in hot and dusty streets', and the coolness and freshness of the dairy were, by suggestion, Hetty's too. A calenture is a feverish thirst; the recurrence of that image here, as a determining factor in Arthur's state of mind at this moment, is one of the ways in which the novel shows his actions as part of a chain of cause and effect. The second sentence of this quotation suggests his state of mind in another way: by reporting his conscious thoughts in such a way that we can see his self-deception. We have seen enough of Arthur already to know the weakness of his resolutions and his habit of deceiving himself about his motives, so that we know that what follows the confident phrase 'Not, of course...' is exactly what he *will* do at the slightest provocation. Hetty's tears are provocation enough. To adopt, after what has passed, 'the air of friendly civility' would require a calm determination that Arthur does not possess, and he would know this if his conscious reasoning were not being distorted by currents under the surface.

After Arthur has kissed Hetty, and she has gone home,

He was feeling much more strongly than he had done in the morning: it was as if his horse had wheeled round from a leap, and dared to dispute his mastery. (135)

What has 'dared to dispute his mastery' is the impulse of tenderness towards Hetty—an impulse that he has underestimated in his conscious assessment of the relationship. The analogy suggests beautifully the amazement and indignation he feels at this rebellion by a part of himself over which he thought he had control. We should not, I think, be misled by the use that, much later, D. H. Lawrence makes of the same comparison, to suggest the rebellion of natural and healthy impulses constricted by the intellect and the will. But the comparison itself must make one consider the possibility (although George Eliot gives it no explicit recognition) that Arthur's sin is not his loving Hetty, but rather his unimaginative failure to consider seriously that he could, in spite of their difference of class, marry her. In its context, however, the resonance of the simile is a different one: it reminds us of the many occasions when Hetty is described in terms of animals, and suggests that Arthur's tenderness towards her is not, in fact, very different in quality from his affection for animals—for his horse, for example:

The pretty creature arched her bay neck in the sunshine, and pawed the gravel, and trembled with pleasure when her master stroked her nose, and patted her, and talked to her even in a more caressing tone than usual.

(303)

He is about to ride in order to overcome his misery about parting from Hetty; and we recall that his first contriving to meet Hetty in the wood was to amuse himself because his horse was lame—

He would amuse himself by seeing Hetty to-day, and get rid of the whole thing from his mind. It was all Irwine's fault. 'If Irwine had said nothing, I shouldn't have thought half so much of Hetty as of Meg's lameness.'

(126)

As for Hetty's part in the guilty relationship, it consists mainly in her excessive trust in Arthur Donnithorne, whom in some respects she takes at his own valuation. Her thoughts are reported:

Captain Donnithorne couldn't like her to go on doing work: he would like to see her in nice clothes, and thin shoes and white stockings, perhaps with silk clocks to them;

(147)

and so he would, we must suppose; and so should we, for George Eliot has described her in such a way that we cannot doubt that 'nice clothes' would show to the best advantage on Hetty—she would delight in them, and be delightful in them. But her thoughts continue:

He would want to marry her, and make a lady of her; she could hardly dare to shape the thought—yet how else could it be?...She didn't know how it could be, but it was quite plain the old Squire could never be told anything about it, for Hetty was ready to faint with awe and fright if she came across him at the Chase...Oh, it was impossible to think how it would be! But Captain Donnithorne would know; he was a great gentleman, and could have his way in everything, and could buy everything he liked.

(147)

The last sentence is Hetty's deduction from Arthur's manner—a perfectly sound deduction concerning Arthur's habitual attitudes towards the world he inhabits. What Hetty is not aware of is Arthur's weakness and the extent to which it imprisons him in the conventions of his class and the expectations of his family. For Hetty is anything but the calculating girl who entraps the young heir into marriage for his money. Her downfall is rather the result of her not being sufficiently calculating to detect the quality of Arthur's tenderness for her. But then, we recall, she has had little experience of tenderness at home—from Mrs Poyser.

It is hard to see how Hetty is to be blamed. Yet George Eliot seems to be determined that we *should* blame her, in the chapter ('The Two Bed-Chambers') in which she is contrasted with Dinah.

> What a strange contrast the two figures made! Visible enough in that mingled twilight and moonlight. Hetty, her cheeks flushed and her eyes glistening from her imaginary drama, her beautiful neck and arms bare, her hair hanging in a curly tangle down her back, and the baubles in her ears. Dinah, covered with her long white dress, her pale face full of subdued emotion, almost like a lovely corpse into which the soul has returned charged with sublimer secrets and a sublimer love. (155)

There is, I think, something that rings false in this description; it gives us, not Hetty and Dinah, but a picture to look at—a painting in the contemporary manner. It might be called 'Sacred and Profane Love', and it might have been painted by, say, Holman Hunt. And the failure of creative imagination in the picture that George Eliot gives us is related to a moral unsureness in the entire chapter.

George Eliot's concern with 'rootedness', the sense of belonging to a place, is effectively and creatively present in *The Mill on the Floss*, but in *Adam Bede* it is not explored critically enough to be anything but confusing. In the later novel we are shown how Maggie Tulliver's pieties are rooted in her recollected childhood, but we can only wonder what strange immorality is being darkly hinted at when we are told of Hetty:

> There are some plants that have hardly any roots: you may tear them from their native nook of rock or wall, and just lay them over your ornamental flower-pot, and they blossom none the worse. Hetty could have cast all her past life behind her, and never cared to be reminded of it again. I think she had no feeling at all towards the old house, and did not like the Jacob's Ladder and the long row of hollyhocks in the garden better than other flowers—perhaps not so well. (151)

In these early chapters, the novelist sometimes seems intent on imposing a moral structure on the world; she seems to need Hetty to be, if not positively wicked, at least in some perceptible degree blameworthy, so that the consequences of her relationship with

Arthur can be regarded as having been brought on by her. But when those consequences do come, they are seen as they really would be, not as they ought to be by any criterion of morality or justice. Hetty's sufferings on her journeys—first in search of Arthur, then, in despair, in search of Dinah—are presented with undistracted sympathy, and George Eliot enters into Hetty's agony with an intensity that leaves considerations of guilt or folly far behind.

There it was, black under the darkening sky: no motion, no sound near. She set down her basket, and then sank down herself on the grass, trembling. The pool had its wintry depth now: by the time it got shallow, as she remembered the pools did at Hayslope, in the summer, no one could find out that it was her body. But then there was her basket—she must hide that too: she must throw it into the water—make it heavy with stones first, and then throw it in. She got up to look about for stones, and soon brought five or six, which she laid down beside her basket, and then sat down again. There was no need to hurry—there was all the night to drown herself in. She sat leaning her elbow on the basket. She was weary, hungry. (370)

No brief sample can adequately suggest the creative achievement of these chapters: it is the sustained steadiness, through many pages, of the novelist's undeviating concern with Hetty's experience that makes them so impressive. It is here that George Eliot is solely and supremely a novelist—that she lays aside all notions, theories, consciously formulated themes, and enters with a whole and awakened imagination into the being of the fictitious character in its fictitious situation. And through this abnegation of deliberate purpose she achieves, more fully than anywhere else in the novel, the deeper purposes that give life to her fiction: to demonstrate the activity of sympathy; to show the tragic dignity of human suffering embodied in such people as we meet every day; and to tell the truth.

So I am content to tell my simple story, without trying to make things seem better than they were; dreading nothing, indeed, but falsity, which, in spite of one's best efforts, there is reason to dread. Falsehood is so easy, truth so difficult...Examine your words well, and you will find that even when you have no motive to be false, it is a very hard thing to say the exact truth, even about your own immediate feelings—much harder than to say something fine about them which is *not* the exact truth. (172)

3

'THE MILL ON THE FLOSS'

In outline, this novel traces the conflict between, on the one hand, individual impulse—all that makes Maggie Tulliver unique—and, on the other, the loyalties and obligations that she has incurred, more or less involuntarily, that have descended upon her. The second, the incurred duties, are embodied in her brother Tom, who represents the family and Maggie's earliest memories; the other forces are shown in her relationship with Philip Wakem, who encourages her intellectual growth and recognizes her right to grow in her own way. As Tom forbids this relationship to go on, and Maggie cannot consent either to disobey him or to terminate the relationship, there is a deadlock which makes it impossible for Maggie's life to blossom in either way. Stephen Guest seems to offer a way out of this deadlock, but, as the way out means breaking faith both with Tom and with Philip, it is an illusion: she had been unable to abandon either, and abandoning both is no solution.

This is, of course, not the only way in which the novel could be briefly described; but I put it in this way in order to confront an important critical question that the novel has raised, and to suggest why I don't find Stephen Guest unsatisfactorily imagined for his function in the novel. One critic, Leslie Stephen, says: 'George Eliot did not herself understand what a mere hairdresser's block she was describing in Mr Stephen Guest.' Disagreeing, Professor Leavis says Stephen is 'sufficiently "there" to give the drama a convincing force'; but he does not object to his being described as a 'provincial dandy,' and writes:

But she has no sense that Stephen Guest (apart, of course, from the in-sufficient strength of moral fibre betrayed under the strain of temptation—and it is to Maggie he succumbs) is not worthy of her spiritual and idealistic nature. There is no hint that, if Fate had allowed them to come together innocently, she wouldn't have found him a pretty satisfactory soulmate;

there, for George Eliot, lies the tragedy—it is conscience opposes. Yet the ordinary nature of the fascination is made quite plain...

But it seems to me that this is precisely what the novel requires; it is an 'ordinary' destiny that Maggie yearns for—very naturally, considering the strenuously extraordinary ones she has otherwise to choose between or hold in precarious suspension. Stephen Guest is indeed an offered escape—but the temptation to escape from the intolerable doesn't deserve our scorn. In fact, of course (but we should be aware that we say 'of course' from our position of safe detachment), the attempt to escape from both sets of obligations is simply a betrayal of both, and as soon as she is able to think clearly Maggie realizes that there can be no rest for such a strenuous soul as hers in an abdication of moral responsibility.

'No—not with my whole heart and soul, Stephen', she said, with timid resolution. 'I have never consented to it with my whole mind. There are memories, and affections, and longing after perfect goodness, that have such a strong hold on me; they would never quit me for long; they would come back and be pain to me—repentance. I couldn't live in peace if I put the shadow of a wilful sin between myself and God. I have caused sorrow already—I know—I feel it; but I have never deliberately consented to it: I have never said, 'They shall suffer, that I may have joy.' It has never been my will to marry you: if you were to win consent from the momentary triumph of my feeling for you, you would not have my whole soul. If I could wake back again into the time before yesterday, I would choose to be true to my calmer affections, and live without the joy of love.' (449)

In spite of the reference, in the hour of choice, to 'sin' and 'God', it is not the Christian religion that provides the overriding sanctions that enforce Maggie's decision not to marry Stephen. The sentence in which she foresees the inescapability of 'repentance' is the one that starts with 'memories', and the major achievement of the novel is to show us what those memories are, what local and familial pieties operate in Maggie, and how these are hardly separable from the sense of her identity.

Maggie's brother Tom, in particular, comes to represent, or to embody, a set of inflexible obligations laid upon Maggie without her choice. It is not the effect of the novel to validate the standards associated with Tom; we are free to feel, and often, I think, we have to feel, that the relationship between Maggie and her brother is a constricting one. We do not, then, have to approve of Maggie's inability to extend her life beyond what Tom might consent to if he understood it properly; but the novel does make us understand how this constriction comes into being. George Eliot said about the novel,

the tragedy is not adequately prepared. This is a defect which I felt even while writing the third volume, and have felt ever since the MS. left me. The Epische Breite into which I was beguiled by love of my subject in the first two volumes, caused a want of proportionate fullness in the treatment of the third, which I shall always regret.

But the proportion seems right. In *Adam Bede*, so little close attention is paid to children that we are brought to contemplate child-murder without thinking of *a child* being murdered, and the Poyser children hardly seem to have human souls. But in *The Mill on the Floss*, the long treatment of Maggie's early years is entirely necessary. It investigates the determining factors in the shaping of character—both the formative influences acting on the child's life, and, through its emphasis on heredity, her inherent and perhaps unalterable characteristics.

Not that we are to take quite seriously the frequent discussions of 'the Dodson blood' and 'the Tulliver blood', which seem, as Maggie's aunts talk, to be inherited fluids that entirely determine the personalities of the children, according to the proportions in which they are mixed.

Still, it was agreed by the sisters, in Mrs. Tulliver's absence, that the Tulliver blood did not mix well with the Dodson blood; that, in fact, poor Bessy's children were Tullivers, and that Tom, notwithstanding he had the Dodson complexion, was likely to be as 'contrairy' as his father. As for Maggie, she was the picture of her Aunt Moss, Mr. Tulliver's sister—a large-boned woman, who had married as poorly as could be; had no china, and had a husband who had much ado to pay his rent. (54)

'"Contrairy" as his father' points to the warmth, spontaneity, even imprudent rashness of Maggie's father. When Mr Tulliver, because he has acted rashly himself, has to reclaim money he has lent to his brother-in-law, he must first 'get into a slight quarrel; it was the most natural and easy introduction to calling in money'.

Poor relations are undeniably irritating—their existence is so entirely un-called for on our part, and they are almost always very faulty people. Mr. Tulliver had succeeded in getting quite as much irritated with Mr. Moss as he had desired, and he was able to say angrily, rising from his seat—

'Well, you must do as you can. *I* can't find money for everybody else as well as myself. I must look to my own business and my own family. I can't lie out o' my money any longer. You must raise it as quick as you can.'

(75)

But as soon as he has refused his sister's invitation to go into the house, and has set off firmly, his natural feelings predominate—those feelings which he had tried to overcome by provoking himself to anger.

No man could feel more resolute till he got outside the yard-gate, and a little way along the deep-rutted lane; but before he reached the next turning, which would take him out of sight of the dilapidated farm-buildings, he appeared to be smitten by some sudden thought. He checked his horse, and made it stand still in the same spot for two or three minutes, during which he turned his head from side to side in a melancholy way, as if he were looking at some painful object on more sides than one. Evidently, after his fit of promptitude, Mr. Tulliver was relapsing into the sense that this is a puzzling world. He turned his horse, and rode slowly back, giving vent to the climax of feeling which had determined this movement by saying aloud, as he struck his horse, 'Poor little wench! she'll have nobody but Tom, belike, when I'm gone.'. . .

'No Gritty, no', said Mr. Tulliver, in a gentle tone. 'Don't you fret—that's all—I'll make a shift without the money a bit—only you must be as cliver and contriving as you can.'

(75)

Tom turns out to be just as puzzled, as far as Latin and Geometry are concerned; but he lacks his father's sense of the puzzling quality of life. There is nothing irresolute or rash about him. He is a Dodson in his unrelenting determination to do what is right and proper, and in his sureness that he knows what is right and proper. Doing what is right, among the Dodsons, follows a set of rigid principles, kept continually aired in their conversation; it does not end with death.

Mrs. Glegg did not alter her will in consequence of this letter, and cut off the Tulliver children from their sixth and seventh share in her thousand pounds; for she had her principles. No one must be able to say of her when she was dead that she had not divided her money with perfect fairness among her own kin: in the matter of wills, personal qualities were subordinate to the great fundamental fact of blood; and to be determined in the distribution of your property by caprice, and not make your legacies bear a direct ratio to degrees of kinship, was a prospective disgrace that would have embittered her life. This had always been a principle in the Dodson family; it was one form of that sense of honour and rectitude which was a proud tradition in such families—a tradition which has been the salt of our provincial society.

(119)

However odd we may find the notion of a life embittered by a 'prospective disgrace' after death (and it is shown to us as an oddity), there is no irony in that final assertion. What the paragraph honours is the firm separation of caprice from principle; and although the Dodson principles are often shown as being capable of excessively serious application to trivial matters, the separation is really a matter of subordinating one's merely personal judgment to a traditional judgment that one knows to be wiser than one's own. Tom fails to make the distinction between caprice and principle: he takes hold of his father's hatred of Wakem, and turns it into a rule of life. In the rigidity of his adherence to it he surpasses the most rigorous Dodson. Mrs Glegg herself could not be more immovably sure of her own rectitude, sanctioned by the tradition of generations, than Tom is of his in adopting his father's resentment as a principle.

But Tom has always been sure that he is right. As a small boy, in combat on a question of heads and tails, in which Tom suspects Bob Jakin of deceit,

Tom fell upon him, threw him down, and got his knees firmly upon Bob's chest.

'You give me the halfpenny now', said Tom.

'Take it', said Bob, sulkily.

'No, I shan't take it; you give it me.'

Bob took the halfpenny out of his pocket and threw it away from him on the ground.

Tom loosed his hold, and left Bob to rise.

'There the halfpenny lies', he said. 'I don't want your halfpenny; I wouldn't have kept it. But you wanted to cheat: I hate a cheat. I shan't go along with you any more', he added, turning round homeward, not without casting a regret towards the rat-catching and other pleasures which he must relinquish along with Bob's society.

(45)

At the end of the chapter, the association of Tom's moral certitude with the incorruptible and severe Rhadamanthus, the judge of the dead in Greek mythology, is both comic as a contribution to the portrayal of the small boy and ominous in relation to Maggie:

> But Tom, you perceive, was rather a Rhadamanthine personage, having more than the usual share of boy's justice in him—the justice that desires to hurt culprits as much as they deserve to be hurt, and is troubled with no doubts concerning the exact amount of their deserts. Maggie saw a cloud on his brow when he came home, which checked her joy at his coming so much sooner than she had expected, and she dared hardly speak to him as he stood silently throwing the small gravel-stones into the mill-dam. It is not pleasant to give up a rat-catching when you have set your mind on it. But if Tom had told his strongest feeling at that moment, he would have said, 'I'd do just the same again.' That was his usual mode of viewing his past actions; whereas Maggie was always wishing she had done something different.　　(46)

For Maggie continually blunders, and there is no forgiveness for blunders in the world that George Eliot portrays here. Hamlet can say—and perhaps Shakespeare says it through him—

> Rashly,—
> And prais'd be rashness for it, let us know,
> Our indiscretion sometimes serves us well
> When our deep plots do pall; and that should teach us
> There's a divinity that shapes our ends,
> Rough-hew them how we will.
>
> (Act v, sc. ii)

But Maggie's indiscretions never seem to serve her well; and that should perhaps teach us that in this novel there is effectively no divinity that shapes people's ends. From Tom, at any rate, there is no mercy. He is entirely Rhadamanthine in his judgment on her failure to feed his rabbits during his absence at school:

> 'You're a naughty girl,' said Tom severely, 'and I'm sorry I bought you the fish-line. I don't love you.'
>
> 'Oh, Tom, it's very cruel', sobbed Maggie. 'I'd forgive you, if *you* forgot anything—I wouldn't mind what you did—I'd forgive you and love you.'
>
> 'Yes, you're a silly—but I never *do* forget things—*I* don't.'
>
> 'Oh, please forgive me, Tom; my heart will break', said Maggie, shaking with sobs, clinging to Tom's arm, and laying her wet cheek on his shoulder.
>
> Tom shook her off, and stopped again, saying in a peremptory tone, 'Now, Maggie, you just listen. Aren't I a good brother to you?'
>
> 'Ye-ye-es', sobbed Maggie, her chin rising and falling convulsedly.
>
> 'Didn't I think about your fish-line all this quarter, and mean to buy it, and saved my money o' purpose, and wouldn't go halves in the toffee, and Spouncer fought me because I wouldn't?'

'Ye-ye-es...and I...lo-lo-love you so, Tom.'

'But you're a naughty girl. Last holidays you licked the paint off my lozenge-box, and the holidays before that you let the boat drag my fish-line down when I'd set you to watch it, and you pushed your head through my kite, all for nothing.'

'But I didn't mean', said Maggie; 'I couldn't help it.'

'Yes, you could,' said Tom, 'if you'd minded what you were doing. And you're a naughty girl, and you shan't go fishing with me to-morrow.'   (30)

This is only one of her many blunders; her childhood seems full of them. There is her impetuous cutting of her hair; her dropping her piece of cake on the floor at Garum Firs; immediately after-wards, her making Tom spill his cowslip wine by impulsively putting her arm round his neck—

Lest you should think it showed a revolting insensibility in Tom that he felt any new anger towards Maggie for this uncalled-for, and, to him, inexplicable caress, I must tell you that he had his glass of cowslip wine in his hand, and that she jerked him so as to make him spill half of it. He must have been an extreme milk-sop not to say angrily, 'Look there, now!' especially when his resentment was sanctioned, as it was, by general disapprobation of Maggie's behaviour.   (85)

Here, as nearly always in this novel, George Eliot's comments on the actions and feelings of the children are fully adult. The novelist takes the children's relationships seriously, and is able to sympathize with them as wholly, and with as mature an intelligence, as with their later adult relationships, without making them seem like little adults. Maggie's clumsiness, which is both the cause and in part the effect of her failure to live up to the requirements of other people (particularly the rigid requirements of the Dodsons and her brother), is important both as a large part of Maggie's experience of childhood, and as a shaping influence on her adult personality, and the novelist gives it its due importance. There is nothing sentimental in such a treatment of childhood. Certainly this novel does not make childhood seem all delightful, a period to which the adult might yearn to go back.

The distortion of childhood comes later, in a few brief retro-spects, perhaps hardly more than rhetorical flourishes. At the end of Book II, when Tom and Maggie return home and their father is ill and financially ruined, George Eliot offers us this closing paragraph:

They had gone forth together into their new life of sorrow, and they would never more see the sunshine undimmed by remembered cares. They had entered the thorny wilderness, and the golden gates of their childhood had for ever closed behind them. (178)

It is as if the novelist has momentarily forgotten, in her eagerness to enrich the moment with an allusion to the expulsion of Adam and Eve from Eden, how thorny Maggie's childhood had been, and how little difference there is, as far as cares are concerned, between the world of Maggie's childhood and that of her adult life. Again, at the end of the novel, as Maggie and Tom are drowned together, we are told:

The boat reappeared—but brother and sister had gone down in an embrace never to be parted: living through again in one supreme moment, the days when they had clasped their little hands in love, and roamed the daisied fields together. (491)

This too is so unlike the texture of childhood as it has been presented in the novel that it looks like sheer fantasy. If that is what it is, it's certainly not just Maggie's fantasy, critically regarded by the author as an illustration of adult illusions about childhood; it is, unfortunately, George Eliot's fantasy. We could, of course, find happy moments in the early part of the novel—but not, I think, moments that could justly be described in these terms—'days when they had clasped their little hands in love, and roamed the daisied fields together'. We could, for example, turn back to the description of Tom and Maggie fishing together.

He threw her line for her, and put the rod into her hand. Maggie thought it probable that the small fish would come to her hook, and the large ones to Tom's. But she had forgotten all about the fish, and was looking dreamily at the glassy water, when Tom said, in a loud whisper, 'Look, look, Maggie!' and came running to prevent her from snatching her line away.

Maggie was frightened lest she had been doing something wrong, as usual, but presently Tom drew out her line and brought a large tench bouncing on the grass. (34)

What this presents, of course, is 'one of their happy mornings'; but Maggie's happiness is severely restricted. It is limited by her sense of her own inferiority in anything she does with Tom— she expects 'that the small fish would come to her hook'—and by her habitual expectation of blame—'Maggie was frightened lest she had been doing something wrong, *as usual.*' This occasion, for Maggie as a child, represents comparative happiness, and the remainder of the chapter erects a weighty structure of generalization upon it. One might suspect that George Eliot had returned to the end of this chapter after writing the end of the novel, and made as much as she could of this moment of moderate happiness, in order that there should after all be *something* memorably pleasant in the shared childhood of Maggie and Tom, for them to remember selectively in the last minutes of their lives.

But the end of the novel, with Tom and Maggie drowning together in the river they have known since their childhood, is not invalidated: it does impress the reader, I think, as being in a sense the culmination and the only fitting end of Maggie's life, although the author's comments do not in this instance help us to see just what the connection is between the shared childhood and the shared death. What the page-by-page texture of the early part of the novel does is to convey vividly the intensity of Maggie's relationship with her brother and with the rest of her childhood environment, and it is this intensity that matters, in the novel, far more than that her childhood should have been predominantly pleasant.

When we come to the part of the novel that deals with Maggie's adult life, our knowledge of her childhood enriches our sense of the complexity of her adult consciousness. It is partly for this reason that the moral consciousness displayed in this novel is so much more complex than in *Adam Bede*. This account of Maggie's changing and conflicting feelings, for example, is considerably more subtle than anything in the earlier novel. It gives the reader a sense of knowing Maggie's mind as he knows his own, largely because he has known her intimately from childhood.

There were moments in which a cruel selfishness seemed to be getting possession of her: why should not Lucy—why should not Philip suffer? *She* had had to suffer through many years of her life; and who had renounced anything for her? And when something like that fulness of existence—love, wealth, ease, refinement, all that her nature craved—was brought within her reach, why was she to forgo it, that another might have it—another, who perhaps needed it less? But amidst all this new passionate tumult there were the old voices making themselves heard with rising power, till, from time to time, the tumult seemed quelled. *Was* that existence which tempted her the full existence she dreamed? Where, then, would be all the memories of early striving, all the deep pity for another's pain, which had been nurtured in her through years of affection and hardship, all the divine presentiment of something higher than mere personal enjoyment which had made the sacredness of life? She might as well hope to enjoy walking by maiming her feet, as hope to enjoy an existence in which she set out by maiming the faith and sympathy that were the best organs of her soul. And then, if pain were so hard to *her*, what was it to others?—'Ah, God! preserve me from inflicting—give me strength to bear it.'—How had she sunk into this struggle with a temptation that she would once have thought herself as secure from, as from deliberate crime? When was that first hateful moment in which she had been conscious of a feeling that clashed with her truth, affection, and gratitude, and had not shaken it from her with horror, as if it had been a loathsome thing?—And yet, since this strange, sweet, subduing influence did not, should not conquer her—since it was to remain simply her own suffering... her mind was meeting Stephen's in that thought of his, that they might still snatch moments of mute confession before the parting came. For was not he suffering too? She saw it daily—saw it in the sickened look of fatigue with which, as soon as he was not compelled to exert himself, he relapsed into indifference towards everything but the possibility of watching her. Could she refuse sometimes to answer that beseeching look which she felt to be following her like a low murmur of love and pain?   (432)

We know those 'years of affection and hardship', those 'old voices' in Maggie that are sometimes able to quell the 'new passionate tumult'. Such moral stability as Maggie has is rooted in the experience of her childhood, and we have shared that experience.

Further, the insight gained into the complexity of adult motives through the novel's long examination of one childhood experience enables the author to deal more confidently with other characters; the study of Maggie is enough to establish the reality of unacknowledged, and even unconscious, motives in other people too—even in the reader.

One other thing Stephen seemed now and then to care for, and that was to sing: it was a way of speaking to Maggie. Perhaps he was not distinctly conscious that he was impelled to it by a secret longing—running counter to all his self-confessed resolves—to deepen the hold he had on her. Watch your own speech, and notice how it is guided by your less conscious purposes, and you will understand that contradiction in Stephen.   (433)

When Maggie has drifted away in a boat with Stephen, she decides to leave him. It is her ultimate indiscretion, for in the eyes of the world she is a fallen woman once she has had the opportunity to fall, and it would be far wiser to go all the way and accept Stephen's invitation of marriage. To put it differently, Maggie here makes a martyr's choice; for she chooses the way of duty when it offers no reward—for herself or for anyone else. The choice is Maggie's supreme heroic folly; it is to such a consummation as this, we see now, that her entire life has been leading.

'Oh, I can't do it', she said, in a voice almost of agony—'Stephen—don't ask me—don't urge me. I can't argue any longer—I don't know what is wise; but my heart will not let me do it. I see—I feel their trouble now: it is as if it were branded on my mind. *I* have suffered, and had no one to pity me; and now I have made others suffer. It would never leave me; it would embitter your love to me. I *do* care for Philip—in a different way: I remember all we said to each other; I know how he thought of me as the one promise of his life. He was given to me that I might make his lot less hard; and I have forsaken him. And Lucy—she has been deceived—she who trusted me more than any one. I cannot marry you: I cannot take a good for myself that has been wrung out of their misery. It is not the force that ought to rule us—this that we feel for each other; it would rend me away from all that my past life has made dear and holy to me. I can't set out on a fresh life, and forget that: I must go back to it, and cling to it, else I shall feel as if there were nothing firm beneath my feet.' (451)

It is no moral philosophy or theory that determines her decision, but a far deeper moral sense, which turns out to be hardly distinguishable from a sense of what she *is*. It is a clear recognition that there is no escape from what she is, however bitterly she might wish there were. It is precisely because this crucial decision is determined by Maggie's recognition of herself—the self fashioned by all her past life—that the novel has had to construct that past life, and especially the texture of her childhood, in such substantial terms. For Maggie, in the moment of choice, 'wisdom' is not relevant: 'I don't know what is wise; but my heart will not let me do it.' And although in her decision there is no appeal to religion, no reference to any divinely sanctioned moral imperative that transcends the human heart's own understanding of itself, we accept the appropriateness of the word 'holy' in 'all that my past life has made dear and holy to me'.

The reality of a religious sense of life suggested here is related, in the novel, to several varieties of Christianity, but it is, in the end, Maggie's own. It is no more to be identified with 'the religion of the Dodsons', which

consisted in revering whatever was customary and respectable: it was necessary to be baptised, else one could not be buried in the churchyard, and to take the sacrament before death as a security against more dimly understood perils; but it was of equal necessity to have the proper pall-bearers and well-cured hams at one's funeral, and to leave an unimpeachable will... (255)

than with Maggie's earlier enthusiasm for Thomas à Kempis's *The Imitation of Christ*:

With all the hurry of an imagination that could never rest in the present, she sat in the deepening twilight forming plans of self-humiliation and entire devotedness; and, in the ardour of first discovery, renunciation seemed to her the entrance into that satisfaction which she had so long been craving in vain. She had not perceived—how could she until she had lived longer? —the inmost truth of the old monk's outpourings, that renunciation remains sorrow, though a sorrow borne willingly. Maggie was still panting for happiness and was in ecstasy because she had found the key to it. (271)

These and other forms of religion that touch Maggie's life are treated more or less ironically; it is not these that give meaning to her use of the word 'holy'. The word derives its force, in the novel, from Maggie's sense of belonging to, being rooted in, a family, a community, and a place. In the act of making a momentous decision, Maggie finds that what resists her personal impulse to escape with Stephen is not a principle of duty, or an idea of Christian renunciation, but a different impulse, a stronger one, within herself—a piety that operates like a passion, over-coming the lesser impulse as no mere principle could. The holiness and the piety have been created in passages like this:

It was when [Mr Tulliver] got able to walk about and look at all the old objects, that he felt the strain of this clinging affection for the old home as part of his life, part of himself. He couldn't bear to think of himself living on any other spot than this, where he knew the sound of every gate and door, and felt that the shape and colour of every roof and weather-stain and broken hillock was good, because his growing senses had been fed on them. (245)

4

'SILAS MARNER'

We have noticed that George Eliot was not entirely satisfied with the structure of *The Mill on the Floss* (see page 21). She felt that the first part of the novel had carried her away, and that she had not left herself room to develop the second part in such a detailed way. We are, of course, free to disagree with her, and to see that novel as having the special value of a work in which the artist's impulse to explore experience over-rides any plan she may have deliberately conceived; we may see it as having its own kind of unity and completeness. But the result of the novelist's dissatisfaction with her earlier novel is the triumph of economy and impersonality that is *Silas Marner*.

What impresses the reader who turns to *Silas Marner* immediately after *The Mill on the Floss* is not, I think, that it is a better novel, but that it is very different from it—almost a different form of art, so that it seems unsatisfactory to call both books simply 'novels'. Perhaps the word 'tale' could be used of the later work, to suggest its conciseness, impersonality and singleness, and its formal affinity with, say, D. H. Lawrence's 'tales' rather than his 'novels'.

In most of George Eliot's novels we can recognize, or suspect, a need to work out some part of her own experience, perhaps to explore possibilities of life that had at some time seemed to be open to her; and we can detect her emotional involvement in one or two characters, so that her struggle to gain our sympathetic comprehension for Maggie Tulliver, or Dorothea Brooke, has something of the pressure of a plea for understanding and sympathy for herself. We may sometimes resist this pressure, but it adds a certain strength to those novels, driving the novelist to exert her intelligence to the utmost in presenting such characters from the inside and making their apparent inconsistencies intelligible to the reader. But in *Silas Marner* she has complete control over her creation; her intelligence is more completely disengaged. Its strength is of a different kind.

Nathaniel Hawthorne called his *The House of the Seven Gables* a 'romance', and the term as he uses it might also be applied to *Silas Marner*. Here is the opening paragraph of Hawthorne's preface:

When a writer calls his work a Romance, it need hardly be observed that he wishes to claim a certain latitude, both as to its fashion and material, which he would not have felt himself entitled to assume had he professed to be writing a Novel. The latter form of composition is presumed to aim at a very minute fidelity, not merely to the possible, but to the probable and ordinary course of man's experience. The former—while, as a work of art, it must rigidly submit itself to laws, and while it sins unpardonably so far as it may swerve aside from the truth of the human heart—has fairly a right to present that truth under circumstances, to a great extent, of the author's own choosing or creation. If he think fit, also, he may so manage his atmospherical medium as to bring out or mellow the lights and deepen and enrich the shadows of the picture. He will be wise, no doubt, to make a very moderate use of the privileges here stated, and, especially, to mingle the Marvellous rather as a slight, delicate and evanescent flavor, than as any portion of the actual substance of the dish offered to the public. He can hardly be said, however, to commit a literary crime even if he disregard this caution.

My concern is not, of course, to find a label for the book, a category into which it can be placed. But if we have in mind the distinctions that Hawthorne makes between a 'Romance' and a 'Novel', we may recognize more clearly the difference between *Silas Marner* and George Eliot's other works of fiction.

It begins—after an introductory paragraph—with this:

In the early years of this century, such a linen-weaver, named Silas Marner, worked at his vocation in a stone cottage that stood among the nutty hedgerows near the village of Raveloe, and not far from the edge of a deserted stone-pit. (2)

The sentence gives us the essential information as compactly and authoritatively as the opening of Chaucer's *Nun's Priest's Tale*:

A povre wydwe, somdeel stape in age,
Was whilom dwellyng in a narwe cotage,
Biside a grove, stondynge in a dale.

It proceeds to this, the closing paragraph of the book:

'O father,' said Eppie, 'what a pretty home ours is! I think nobody could be happier than we are.' (246)

—which, as a conclusion, can hardly be—and is certainly not offered by George Eliot as—minutely faithful to 'the probable and ordinary course of man's experience'; it is much nearer to the traditional ending of a story for children: 'and they lived happily ever after'.

The crucial event in the story is the appearance in Silas's cottage—not long after the loss of his gold—of a little girl, whose mother has died in the snow. Silas, who has just undergone one of his occasional attacks of catalepsy but does not know it, has not seen the child come in.

Turning towards the hearth, where the two logs had fallen apart, and sent forth only a red uncertain glimmer, he seated himself on his fireside chair, and was stooping to push his logs together, when, to his blurred vision, it seemed as if there were gold on the floor in front of the hearth. Gold!—his own gold—brought back to him as mysteriously as it had been taken away! He felt his heart begin to beat violently, and for a few moments he was unable to stretch out his hand and grasp the restored treasure. The heap of gold seemed to glow and get larger beneath his agitated gaze. He leaned forward at last, and stretched forth his hand; but instead of the hard coin with the familiar resisting outline, his fingers encountered soft warm curls. In utter amazement, Silas fell on his knees and bent his head low to examine the marvel: it was a sleeping child—a round, fair thing, with soft yellow rings all over its head. (151)

Clearly George Eliot does not suggest, or suppose, that life is commonly found to be like this. The scene, with its fully explicit symbolism, is offered as an image of the process the book presents: the substitution of the child for the lost gold summarizes, or crystallizes, in a frankly 'contrived' scene, the transfer of Silas's affections from his sterile hoard of gold to the child who gives him a new and living relationship with the people among whom he lives.

But, despite the book's freedom from the usual constraints of the 'realistic' novel, it has its own very firm grasp of reality. Dunstan Cass's thoughts, when he enters the weaver's cottage and finds nobody there, are rendered with full attention to the question of how *that* mind, a rather stupid one, would really work in that situation—

If the weaver was dead, who had a right to his money? Who would know where his money was hidden? *Who would know that anybody had come to take it away*? He went no farther into the subtleties of evidence: the pressing question, 'Where *is* the money?' now took such entire possession of him as to make him quite forget that the weaver's death was not a certainty. A dull mind, once arriving at an inference that flatters a desire, is rarely able to retain the impression that the notion from which the inference started was purely problematic. (49)

If this book is a tale, a romance, or even a parable, it is evidently not merely a story in which allegorical figures move in an allegorical landscape. George Eliot's mind is continually revealing its habitual curiosity about why people behave as they do, and implying in the account of any one person's motives some more or less general comment on the way *our* minds work.

Mr. Snell was correct in his surmise, that somebody else would remember the pedlar's ear-rings. For, on the spread of inquiry among the villagers, it was stated with gathering emphasis, that the parson had wanted to know whether the pedlar wore ear-rings in his ears, and an impression was created that a great deal depended on the eliciting of this fact. Of course every one who heard the question, not having any distinct image of the pedlar as *without* ear-rings, immediately had an image of him *with* ear-rings, larger or smaller, as the case might be; and the image was presently taken for a vivid recollection, so that the glazier's wife, a well-intentioned woman, not given to lying, and whose house was among the cleanest in the village, was ready to declare, as sure as ever she meant to take the sacrament, the very next Christmas that was ever coming, that she had seen big ear-rings, in the shape of the young moon, in the pedlar's two ears; while Jinny Oates, the cobbler's daughter, being a more imaginative person, stated not only that she had seen them too, but that they made her blood creep, as it did at that very moment while there she stood. (83)

The process by which a question can, so to speak, generate an answer, and an image turn into a certain recollection, is fully imagined—so fully that the very turns of phrase used by the people involved penetrate the narrative prose. The observed absurdity of the way in which people emphasize their certainty of uncertain facts, by insistent accentuation of circumstantial irrelevancies, is incorporated into the texture of the description— 'the very next Christmas that was ever coming', 'at that very moment while there she stood'.

The 'romance', then, with its flavour of the marvellous, involves no thinness in the texture of reality, no relaxation of the author's grasp of the way things happen in the actual world.

Everywhere in the quality of its prose this book displays that awareness of the way people do react, and that sympathetic and intellectual curiosity that we are accustomed to find in George Eliot's other works; that impulse to unite the particular observation and the general laws of human nature that so often expresses itself in some variant of the phrases 'Have we not all...' or 'Which of us has not...'. Godfrey Cass is anxiously waiting for his brother to return—

Instead of trying to still his fears, he encouraged them, with that superstitious impression which clings to us all, that if we expect evil very strongly it is the less likely to come... (85)

—and the same consideration that makes Godfrey's state of mind intelligible to us has at the same time made us see a characteristic of our own, and perhaps of mankind. Sometimes the conjectured generalization may be more explicit, but it always seems to grow out of the particular incident that is being explained; here is Godfrey Cass, much later in the book:

Meanwhile, why could he not make up his mind to the absence of children from a hearth brightened by such a wife? Why did his mind fly uneasily to that void, as if it were the sole reason why life was not thoroughly joyous to him? I suppose it is the way with all men and women who reach middle age without the clear perception that life never *can* be thoroughly joyous: under the vague dulness of the grey hours, dissatisfaction seeks a definite object, and finds it in the privation of an untried good. (214)

This discontent, in some measure, is a consequence of growing older, and that it is both unreasonable and inevitable that one tends to attach to some specific lack this discontent that was not originally the consequence of anything specific, is an observation that simultaneously leads us to understand Godfrey's feelings sympathetically and invites us to consider our own critically.

However *Silas Marner* may differ, then, from the author's other fictions, it is always quite recognizably hers. The relations I have indicated, in the texture of the prose, between the generalizing intelligence and the particularizing imagination, is characteristic of all her novels. Her concern, in this book, with the relation between a man and the community in which he is rooted, is also recognizable as one of her habitual preoccupations.

It is treated here with a detachment that marks an advance from the sentimental treatment of the Poyser's distress at the prospect of moving to another parish, in *Adam Bede,* and even from the demonstration of the power of rootedness in Maggie Tulliver, in *The Mill on the Floss*—which, masterly as it is, makes no pretence of objectivity.

Silas makes his first appearance as one of

> certain pallid undersized men, who, by the side of the brawny country-folk, looked like the remnants of a disinherited race. (1)

The tale is to be about his recovery of his inheritance—his inheritance as a man, a social being. But it is not only Silas's incapacity for making full human contact with the people around him that alienates him from the country people of Raveloe. We are given the causes of that incapacity very soon—the account of the events that have led to his loss of faith and his removal to Raveloe; but what the first paragraphs of the novel give us, with generalizing precision, is the incapacity of the Raveloe people for accepting the stranger. The traditional wisdom of a rooted rural community has, evidently, its own constricting limitations.

> In that far-off time superstition clung easily round every person or thing that was at all unwonted, or even intermittent and occasional merely, like the visits of the pedlar or the knife-grinder. No one knew where wandering men had their homes or their origin; and how was a man to be explained unless you at least knew somebody who knew his father and mother? (1)

The country people of Raveloe are, of course, the community in which, if anywhere, Silas must find his place and his identity; but we are not allowed to suppose that they have any special virtues merely because they *are* a rural community. Silas has himself been a member of an urban community; he has been driven out of it, as an innocent man may be driven out of any society in which a less innocent man may seek his own advantage at his expense, but it has been a real community in which an individual had his place and could form and establish his own identity.

> His life, before he came to Raveloe, had been filled with the movement, the mental activity, and the close fellowhip, which, in that day as in this, marked the life of an artisan early incorporated in a narrow religious sect, where the

poorest layman has the chance of distinguishing himself by gifts of speech, and has, at the very least, the weight of a silent voter in the government of his community. (7)

It has been, too, a place where his deepest pieties were anchored, as Maggie Tulliver's had been in and around St Ogg's and the Mill: it is not only a rural community that can provide this stability. In fact, for Silas, Raveloe is at first a place without meaning, a place where he is disinherited:

> There was nothing here, when he rose in the deep morning quiet and looked out on the dewy brambles and rank tufted grass, that seemed to have any relation with that life centering in Lantern Yard, which had once been to him the altar-place of high dispensations. The white-washed walls; the little pews where well-known figures entered with a subdued rustling, and where first one well-known voice and then another, pitched in a peculiar key of petition, uttered phrases at once occult and familiar, like the amulet worn on the heart; the pulpit where the minister delivered unquestioned doctrine, and swayed to and fro, and handled the book in a long-accustomed manner; the very pauses between the couplets of the hymn, as it was given out, and the recurrent swell of voices in song: these things had been the channel of divine influences to Marner—they were the fostering home of his religious emotions—they were Christianity and God's kingdom upon earth.
>
> (17)

'The dewy brambles'—this is not, we feel, Silas's observation, but the artist's comment, hinting at the refreshment to be found in the beauty of the countryside; 'rank tufted grass', too, is a description that suggests an observer accustomed to noticing different kinds and qualities of grasses, not Silas; and even 'deep morning quiet' is an appreciative phrase that, with the others I have mentioned, shows through familiar and loving eyes the rural scene that is for him unfamiliar and unloved. For Silas, these things are merely the absence of the world he has known, with as little attraction or emotional significance for him as the scenes of his childhood would have for us. It is perhaps a certain sentimentality in us, or many of us, that makes it so much easier for us to imagine somebody being emotionally rooted—bound and sustained by links of memory—in a rural environment, among 'dewy brambles and rank tufted grass', than in an urban one like the Lantern Yard. Even if our own early memories have been urban, we seem to have little difficulty in imagining the 'rootedness' of a country man. What George Eliot does in this passage is to suggest, and make accessible to our imagination, the 'rootedness' of a town-dweller of a rather special kind—a 'rootedness' that her readers are not likely to have experienced, and are certainly not accustomed to finding depicted in fiction. She makes it irrelevant, for the moment, that we are accustomed to think of 'narrow religious sects' such as the one Silas belonged to as fanatical organizations, led by visionaries either insane or dishonest, exploiting the ignorance and emotional poverty of the new urban proletariat. All this they might be, and the brief account George Eliot gives of the events that led to Silas's departure is an unsparing, though compassionate, indictment of them. But even there—this is what the quoted passage makes us realize—even there a man's childhood memories and his deepest pieties might be rooted. The series of phrases conveying the texture of Silas's recollected childhood has its own rhythm—a rhythm that suggests the mind groping in its past, and bringing out a sequence of broken images, precious because they are what one's consciousness and one's identity is made of—and these phrases ('The white-washed walls; the little pews...') themselves become for us 'phrases at once occult and familiar, like the amulet worn on the heart'.

When we have recognized the artistic triumph of this concise creation, however, it is in rural Raveloe that we trace Silas's re-planting in the course of the book. This process begins before the arrival of the child; Silas's neighbours begin to take an interest in him, as a man who has suffered, after his gold has been stolen. Dolly Winthrop visits him, with a gift of cakes, to urge him to go to church, and their dialogue is a series of misunderstandings. We have been given enough insight into what religion has meant to Silas, and what it means in Raveloe, to be aware of the near impossibility of communication between the two; that is, we are perfectly able to understand Dolly Winthrop, and at the same time able to see how unintelligible her words are to Silas.

'Well, Master Marner, it's niver too late to turn over a new leaf, and if you've niver had no church, there's no telling the good it'll do you. For I feel so set up and comforable as niver was, when I've been and heard the prayers, and the singing to the praise and glory o' God, as Mr. Macey gives out—and Mr. Crackenthorp saying good words, and more partic'lar on Sacramen' Day; and if a bit o' trouble comes, I feel as I can put up wi' it, for I've looked for help i' the right quarter, and gev myself up to Them as we must all give ourselves up to at the last; and if we'n done our part, it isn't to be believed as Them as are above us 'ull be worse nor we are, and come short o' Theirn.'

(112)

It is entirely characteristic of the secure poise of the book that we laugh without mockery at Dolly Winthrop's 'simple Raveloe theology', recognizing it as something of value that she possesses and Silas lacks.

He continues to lack it for the time being; the loss of his gold has not been enough to bring him into full contact with his neighbours, although it has been a necessary preparation. After Eppie's arrival, Dolly Winthrop renews the attack, and her theology is still as unintelligible to Silas as before, but now she can appeal not only to Silas's own need but to his obligation to the child.

'And it's my belief', she went on, 'as the poor little creatur has never been christened, and it's nothing but right as the parson should be spoke to...for if the child ever went anyways wrong, and you hadn't done your part by it, Master Marner,—'noculation, and everything to save it from harm—it 'ud be a thorn i' your bed for ever o' this side the grave... (169)

Again we may smile at Mrs Winthrop's simple-minded view of baptism, which she urges upon Silas as a preventive measure of mysterious nature and doubtful efficacy against spiritual harm of an unspecified kind, and links with inoculation against smallpox. But the value of her urging does not depend on the efficacy of either treatment: it lies in her concern for the child and for Silas, and in her willingness to teach Silas what he must do in order to give the child the best care he can. It is in care for the child that Silas is able to meet Mrs Winthrop and the other Raveloe people; he is eager to do for Eppie what he was earlier uninterested in doing for himself.

'But I want to do everything as can be done for the child. And whatever's right for it i' this country, and you think 'ull do it good, I'll act according, if you'll tell me.' (169)

Finding himself, after fifteen years of mere existence, involves for Silas something like learning a new language; he has to learn to understand Mrs Winthrop's way of talking, and this is only a part of learning what life means in Raveloe. But it also involves finding ways of talking to Mrs Winthrop about his own past,

necessarily a slow and difficult process, for Silas's meagre power of explanation was not aided by any readiness of interpretation in Dolly, whose narrow outward experience gave her no key to strange customs, and made every novelty a source of wonder that arrested them at every step of the narrative.

(192)

The difficulties are not merely noted: they are made vividly—and amusingly—real to us in Dolly Winthrop's speech, which Silas gradually comes to understand. The dialogue between them is, at the same time, a dialogue between Raveloe and the Lantern Yard, and between Silas's new and old lives; the gradual approach to comprehension between them traces the gradual healing of the breach in Silas's life. The healing culminates—it is made to seem inevitable—in his re-visiting the town where he spent his childhood and youth, and taking Eppie with him.

'The old place is all swep' away,' Silas said to Dolly Winthrop on the night of his return—'the little graveyard and everything. The old home's gone; I've no home but this now.'

(241)

The point is not, I think, that the rapidity of change in a town, compared with rural permanence, makes it an unfavourable place to have roots in. It is to be taken symbolically: Silas has found, as in some sense we must all find, that his past is no longer there to go back to; his 'roots' (the simple metaphor is clearly inadequate for the concept here seen in complex terms) in order to sustain him must cling to the future, for the past has gone.

Meanwhile the story of Godfrey Cass, Eppie's 'real' father, necessary at first to justify the marvel of Eppie's coming from nowhere into Silas's life and to give this a causal connection as well as a symbolic one with the theft of the gold, has itself grown into a concurrent theme. As Silas's cottage becomes a home through his acceptance of the abandoned child, Godfrey's large red house remains childless.

Godfrey's story develops several of the same pre-occupations that George Eliot has already begun to explore in her treatment of Arthur Donnithorne in *Adam Bede*. Godfrey learns, when he offers to acknowledge Eppie as his daughter and take her to his home, that

—'there's debts we can't pay like money debts, by paying extra for the years that have slipped by. While I've been putting off and putting off, the trees have been growing—it's too late now...I wanted to pass for childless once, Nancy—I shall pass for childless now against my wish.'

(236)

His interview with Eppie and Silas, which has led him to this conclusion, has been strictly faithful to what Hawthorne calls 'the truth of the human heart', with Godfrey's awkwardness continually betraying the fact that he is not at all sure whether he is begging or conferring a favour. George Eliot presents, in her account of that visit, what such a man as Godfrey really would feel and say—not what, in a novel (or romance) one would expect him to feel and say.

Godfrey felt an irritation inevitable to almost all of us when we encounter an unexpected obstacle. He had been full of his own penitence and resolution to retrieve his error as far as the time was left to him; he was possessed with all-important feelings, that were to lead to a predetermined course of action which he had fixed on as the right, and he was not prepared to enter with lively appreciation into other people's feelings counteracting his virtuous resolves.

(228)

There is no easy assurance that all would have been well for Godfrey if he had acknowledged the child—and his drunken and drug-addicted first wife—openly from the start. Nancy suggests it, and the suggestion itself is painful and perhaps salutary to Godfrey:

'And—O, Godfrey—if we'd had her from the first, if you'd taken to her as you ought, she'd have loved me for her mother—and you'd have been happier with me: I could better have bore my little baby dying, and our life might have been more like what we used to think it 'ud be.'

(220)

But Godfrey's answer, though 'urged in the bitterness of his self-reproach, to prove to himself that his conduct had not been utter folly', is convincing:

'But you wouldn't have married me then, Nancy, if I'd told you... You may think you would now, but you wouldn't then. With your pride and your father's, you'd have hated having anything to do with me after the talk there'd have been.' (220)

Judging from all we have seen of Nancy Lammeter, this is true; and she does not deny it. And if, as we have seen, Godfrey's discontent can fix upon the lack of children because that is all he lacks, it is unlikely that his discontent would have been without an object if he had had the child and not married Nancy. Since the speculation about what might have been arises in the story itself, we may be justified in taking it a little further: Godfrey with Eppie, unsuccessful in winning Nancy (who would nevertheless not marry anybody else), living in the dismal, unreformed Red House (supposing he had the luck not to be disinherited) would have real cause for gloom; and in such an atmosphere Eppie (under another name) would have grown up. One can hardly suppose that anybody would be better off as a result.

But in order to recognize the consequences of one's wrongdoing, it is not necessary to be able to see precisely how, at any given stage, one could have acted otherwise so as to make all well. Godfrey has disowned his daughter, and remained childless; finally his daughter disowns him. For Godfrey at least, the link between his action and its sequel is a moral link: he is punished.

For the world of *Silas Marner*, for all its marvels, is a moral world; for all the coincidences that go to conceal Godfrey's first marriage, it is not a fairy-tale world in which coincidence can legitimately be counted on to get one out of messes of one's own making. Early in the novel we are told of him,

He fled to his usual refuge, that of hoping for some unforeseen turn of fortune, some favourable chance which would save him from unpleasant consequences —perhaps even justify his insincerity by manifesting its prudence. (99)

The unforeseen turns of fortune come—the acknowledged wife dies, his brother disappears, and his child survives and is well looked after—but none of these manifestations of the 'prudence' of his deceit can justify it or avert its consequences in his heart. The consequences are hidden, mysterious and organic, as George Eliot's image suggests: 'the orderly sequence by which the seed brings forth a crop after its kind'.

5

'FELIX HOLT'

The question 'What is it about?' is likely to perplex the reader more in this novel than in any of the others. The painstaking and restless ingenuity of the plot, supported at nearly every point with explanations of the motives of the numerous people involved and with justifications of the frequent coincidences, makes the focus of attention uncertain; there are parts of the novel that look like exercises in demonstrating the inevitability of the improbable.

In such a difficulty, we owe George Eliot the courtesy of trying, at least, to follow the indication she gives us in the title: *Felix Holt, the Radical*. If we take Felix as the centre, the novel takes some such shape as this.

Felix Holt's radicalism begins at home, where it is most painful: he will not allow his mother to 'live by the sale of medicines whose virtues he distrusts'. 'It is', says Rufus Lyon, 'no common scruple.' He identifies himself with working men:

'I would never choose to withdraw myself from the labour and common burthen of the world; but I do choose to withdraw myself from the push and the scramble for money and position. Any man is at liberty to call me a fool, and say that mankind are benefited by the push and the scramble in the long-run. But I care for the people who live now and will not be living when the long-run comes. As it is, I prefer going shares with the unlucky.'

(241)

In all this he contrasts sharply with Harold Transome, whose radicalism operates principally on the level of party-politics—in which he employs, with only ineffectual protest against having to know about it, agents whose virtues he distrusts—and perhaps on the level of estate management, where he likes to get to the bottom of things. But Harold has no intention of giving up any of the privileges of wealth and position; in fact he chooses his political party to safeguard that wealth and position by swimming with the current. Felix is radical by temperament and on prin-

43

ciple; his radicalism tackles social evils at the root, in educating the young; and in his other occupation as a repairer and cleaner of clocks, he might almost be seen as the emblematic type of the reformer of institutions.

Yet he is not a reformer of institutions. In fact, in modern political terms, he is a reactionary; his belief that the mechanical reform of institutions is of no use without the reform of the individual coincides with an argument against political change that is thoroughly familiar today and was hardly original in 1830 when the action of the novel takes place. The conservative Samuel Johnson had written in 1764, in lines contributed to Goldsmith's *The Traveller*,

> How small, of all that human hearts endure,
> The part which laws or kings can cause or cure.
> Still to ourselves in every place consign'd,
> Our own felicity we make or find.

The place for radical reform, for Felix, is the heart, not Parliament. He has, himself, been 'converted by six weeks' debauchery'.

'If I had not seen that I was making a hog of myself very fast, and that pig-wash, even if I could have got plenty of it, was a poor sort of thing, I should never have looked life fairly in the face to see what was to be done with it. I laughed out loud at last to think of a poor devil like me, in a Scotch garret, with my stockings out at heel and a shilling or two to be dissipated upon, with a smell of raw haggis mounting from below, and old women breathing gin as they passed me on the stairs—wanting to turn my life into easy pleasure. Then I began to see what else it could be turned into. Not much, perhaps. This world is not a very fine place for a good many of the people in it. But I've made up my mind it shan't be the worse for me, if I can help it...'

(57)

As a result, he is prepared to regulate his own life like a well-cleaned clock, and to try, whenever an opportunity appears, to make others see the folly of their lives as he has seen the folly of his.

'I'll never marry, though I should have to live on raw turnips to subdue my flesh. I'll never look back and say, "I had a fine purpose once—I meant to keep my hands clean, and my soul upright, and to look truth in the face; but pray excuse me, I have a wife and children—I must lie and simper a little, else they'll starve"; or, "My wife is nice, she must have her bread well buttered, and her feelings will be hurt if she is not thought genteel". That is the lot Miss Esther is preparing for some man or other...I should like to see if she could be made ashamed of herself.' (68)

'To keep my hands clean'—the ambition is entirely characteristic of the man. Without going so far as to suggest that political power—the power to bring about reforms—cannot be obtained without employing such methods as Harold condones, we may reasonably see Felix's central concerns as incompatible with political effectiveness. His solidarity with what he regards as his class is for the sake of his own integrity rather than for any good he can do to that class, although Felix allows of no distinction between the two aims.

'Why should I want to get into the middle class because I have some learning? ...That's how the working men are left to foolish devices and keep worsening themselves: the best heads among them forsake their born comrades, and go in for a house with a high doorstep and a brass knocker.' (59)

When Rufus Lyon suggests an opposite view—

'Nevertheless...it is by such self-advancement that many have been enabled to do good service to the cause of liberty and to the public well-being' (59)

—Felix has no reply to offer except an indignant repudiation, for his own part, of the idea of becoming one of 'your ringed and scented men of the people'.

It will be clear that his 'radicalism' is a blend of earthy common sense, vehement moral indignation, and a certain force and facility in rhetoric—both in talking to himself and in talking to others. A good deal of the novel is concerned with his efforts to communicate some of his common sense and seriousness to Esther, who resists with a spiritedness that makes her a fit adversary for him.

'That's what makes women a curse; all life is stunted to suit their littleness. That's why I'll never love, if I can help it; and if I love, I'll bear it, and never marry.'...
  'I ought to be very much obliged to you for giving me your confidence so freely.'
  'Ah! now you are offended with me, and disgusted with me. I expected it would be so. A woman doesn't like a man who tells her the truth.'
  'I think you boast a little too much of your truth-telling, Mr. Holt', said Esther, flashing out at last. 'That virtue is apt to be easy to people when they only wound others and not themselves. Telling the truth often means no more than taking a liberty.' (115)

There is enough conviction behind such comments as Esther's to make it clear that George Eliot is not offering Felix for our unqualified admiration. But he is certainly a focus of interest in large parts of the novel; he has a certain force, and however improbable some of his speeches may be, he is undeniably a presence in the novel. One test that seems to me to confirm this is here—when Esther goes to visit Felix in prison:

Esther automatically took off her gloves and bonnet, as if she had entered the house after a walk. She had lost the complete consciousness of everything except that she was going to see Felix. She trembled. It seemed to her as if he too would look altered after her new life—as if even the past would change for her and be no longer a steadfast remembrance, but something she had been mistaken about, as she had been about the new life. Perhaps she was growing out of that childhood to which common things have rareness, and all objects look larger. Perhaps from henceforth the whole world was to be meaner for her. The dread concentrated in those moments seemed worse than anything she had known before. It was what the dread of a pilgrim might be who has it whispered to him that the holy places are a delusion, or that he will see them with a soul unstirred and unbelieving. Every minute that passes may be charged with some such crisis in the little inner world of man or woman.

But soon the door opened slightly; some one looked in; then it opened wide, and Felix Holt entered.

'Miss Lyon—Esther!' and her hand was in his grasp.

He was just the same—no, something inexpressibly better, because of the distance and separation, and the half-weary novelties, which made him like the return of morning. (400)

This seems to me to be convincingly real in its context, in a way in which the asserted radiance of Ladislaw in *Middlemarch* is not real. An important part of the context is the absence of Felix from the preceding hundred pages of the novel; in the meantime Esther has gained experience that has given, for her and for the reader, substantial meaning to the things that Felix had been trying to tell her. His vehement condemnations of Fine Ladyism had been too abstract, too remote from Esther's experience and from anything concretely presented in the novel in relation to Esther, for us to take them very seriously; but while Felix has been in prison Esther has had to make a choice. She has found that she can have Transome Court for the taking, with or without Harold Transome: all the coincidences and legalities have been contrived to put her in that position. Mrs Transome *is* the Fine Lady; and despite Esther's great sympathy with her as a suffering woman, she cannot wish to be her daughter and successor. All she has wished for in daydreams has been offered to her, and she finds the reality unglamorous. Perhaps she would not have found it so, if Felix had not prepared her to doubt the value of her daydream.

So Felix has gained in reality and convincingness in his absence; and it is what he means to Esther that gives him his reality for us (rather as the ghost in *Hamlet* is convincing because of the effect it has on Horatio, Marcellus and Hamlet, rather than because of its own dim presence). Yet we have to recognize that Felix *has* been shown in his own person, even in his own consciousness, so that we can recognize this paragraph as a development of his character and not merely an idea of the author's put in his mouth:

'No, you are dreadfully inspired', said Felix. 'When the wicked tempter is tired of snarling that word failure in a man's cell, he sends a voice like a thrush to say it for him. See now what a messenger of darkness you are!' He smiled, and took her two hands between his, pressed together as children hold them up in prayer. Both of them felt too solemnly to be bashful. They looked straight into each other's eyes, as angels do when they tell some truth. And they stood in that way while he went on speaking. (401)

Yet, however convincing Felix becomes by the end of the novel, we can't take him quite seriously in his earlier appearances. If one reads his speeches aloud, one has difficulty in finding a consistent tone for them; George Eliot seems to have made them up, not imaginatively heard them.

'You are thoroughly mistaken', said Felix. 'It is just because I'm a very ambitious fellow, with very hungry passions, wanting a great deal to satisfy me, that I have chosen to give up what people call worldly good. At least that has been one determining reason. It all depends on what a man gets into his consciousness—what life thrusts into his mind, so that it becomes present to him as remorse is present to the guilty, or a mechanical problem to an inventive genius...' (242)

—Why doesn't it sound right? We might guess that the structure of the last sentence of the quotation is unlikely to occur in speech; or that the brisk casualness of the interpolated definition ('What

life thrusts into his mind') is hard to reconcile with the prompt
occurrence of the two analogies in the end of the sentence. But
perhaps such things *can* happen in speech; that is not the point.
Whether they can or not, George Eliot does not convince us that
they do. She has considered, reflected, and concluded that such a
man would speak in such a way; but she has not, with an awakened
imagination, *heard* him doing so. If she had, his tone would have
commanded assent—we should have recognized it.

What I have so far said about the unreality of Felix's speech
could be applied to large parts of *Romola*. But there is a special
failure of consistency in Felix, besides the weakness that indicates, generally, a weakening of the novelist's grasp. This is the
ambiguity of Felix's class. He wants to live in solidarity with the
class in which he sees his origin, despite a superior education.
It is a perfectly credible wish, and a difficult one to fulfil; and if
Felix is unable to maintain any effective communication with the
class he thinks he belongs to, this could well be presented,
sympathetically, as a failure that many educated people have
experienced. But George Eliot is here evidently quite unaware
that it *is* a failure she is displaying. This is Felix offering political
education to the workers, in the tavern at Sproxton:

'Should you like to know all about the Reform?' said Felix, using his
opportunity. 'If you would, I can tell you.'
'Ay, ay—tell's; you know, I'll be bound', said several voices at once.
'Ah, but it will take some little time. And we must be quiet. The cleverest
of you—those who are looked up to in the club—must come and meet me at
Peggy Button's cottage next Saturday, at seven o'clock, after dark. And,
Brindle, you must bring that little yellow-haired lad of yours. And anybody
that's got a little boy—a very little fellow, who won't understand what is
said—may bring him. But you must keep it close, you know. We don't want
fools there. But everybody who hears me may come. I shall be at Peggy
Button's.'
(125)

Our criticism must be, surely, not only that George Eliot has
failed to give Felix any convincing sense of political tactics, but
that she has hardly given any imaginative thought at all to the
question. So we have Felix inviting a selection of the workers, in
extremely tactless terms ('The cleverest of you—those who are
looked up to in the club'), and a few sentences later making the

invitation an open one. In the suggestion that Brindle should bring his son Felix is carrying out the tactical plan conceived beforehand—

'I'll lay hold of them by their fatherhood', said Felix; 'I'll take one of their little fellows and set him in the midst...' (121)

But in the next breath he extends his invitation, too, to 'anybody that's got a little boy—a very little fellow, who won't understand what is said'. Now the initial plan was not original; it was adopted whimsically from Jesus ('And he took a child, and set him in the midst of them...'—*Matthew*, Chapter IX); but the modified plan seems utterly, and disastrously, unconsidered—it threatens to engulf the projected meeting in a welter of uncomprehending infants.

I need not labour the point. Felix, as a political figure in the novel, does not begin to exist. And although he is real enough as a force in Esther's life, he is not the artistic centre of the novel—the point at which the novelist's creative imagination makes discoveries. That centre, it seems to me, is in Mrs Transome.

Mrs Transome is fully and finely presented, wholly imagined, from her first appearance in the novel.

She saw nothing else: she was not even conscious that the small group of her own servants had mustered, or that old Hickes the butler had come forward to open the chaise door. She heard herself called 'Mother!' and felt a light kiss on each cheek; but stronger than all that sensation was the consciousness which no previous thought could prepare her for, that this son who had come back to her was a stranger. Three minutes before, she had fancied that, in spite of all changes wrought by fifteen years of separation, she should clasp her son again as she had done at their parting; but in the moment when their eyes met, the sense of strangeness came upon her like a terror. It was not hard to understand that she was agitated, and the son led her across the hall to the sitting-room, closing the door behind them. Then he turned towards her and said, smiling—

'You would not have known me, eh, mother?' (13)

When, very soon after this, Mrs Transome is alone and weeps, the novelist has not at all satisfactorily *explained* why she does so, but the reader knows. It is the mark of the novelist's success that she doesn't need to explain.

A dramatist, it has been said—and it could be said of a novelist too—need not understand people: but he must be exceptionally aware of them. What George Eliot is here exceptionally aware of, and makes us vividly sense, is the abrupt presence of the strangeness, the terror, that Harold is. It is made real for us very quickly, after the passage I have quoted, in the tones of his voice, though he says little—tones that warn us at once to despair of his ever entering into a full sympathetic relationship with his mother. One way of describing this certainty would be to say that the sensibility he reveals is a coarse one; but that would perhaps suggest too strongly that Mrs Transome's sensibility is a refined and delicate one. It isn't at all so; she is accustomed to dominate, as we have seen in her husband's terror of her—

> But when Mrs. Transome appeared within the doorway, her husband paused in his work and shrank like a timid animal looked at in a cage where flight is impossible. He was conscious of a troublesome intention, for which he had been rebuked before—that of disturbing all his specimens with a view to a new arrangement. (11)

And a certain toughness in her character, built up through the years of waiting for her son's return, is evident in the closing lines of the chapter:

> and now that she had seen him, she said to herself, in her bitter way, 'It is a lucky eel that escapes skinning. The best happiness I shall ever know, will be to escape the worst misery.' (27)

It isn't at all a delicacy and refinement in Mrs Transome that makes us shudder at her son's 'gay carelessness' of manner; it's the fact—clearly present in all we see of her even more vividly than in what we are told of her—that she has kept one 'access and passage' to tenderness in the hard shell that she has presented all those years to a gossiping and pitying world: and Harold's good-natured egoism is never going to find it. Although, once more paying tribute to the novelist's dramatic power, I have said we feel this more vividly than George Eliot explicitly tells us of it, yet she *does* tell us of it—this concealed vulnerability and possible accessibility to tenderness as well as to pain, behind Mrs Transome's hard, strong manner; at the end of the chapter she tells us of it in a poetic image that is more communicative than any amount of psychological explanation.

Mrs. Transome found the opiate for her discontent in the exertion of her will about smaller things...If she had only been more haggard and less majestic, those who had glimpses of her outward life might have said she was a tyrannical, griping harridan, with a tongue like a razor. No one said exactly that; but they never said anything like the full truth about her, or divined what was hidden under that outward life—a woman's keen sensibility and dread, which lay screened behind all her petty habits and narrow notions, as some quivering thing with eyes and throbbing heart may be crouching behind withered rubbish. (26)

The movement of the prose here is entirely characteristic of George Eliot at her most fully creative; it is the characteristic movement of her mind in its creative leaps. In the first sentence, and several that I have omitted, she takes us as far as observation and deduction can go towards describing Mrs Transome's character: she respects rationality, explicitness, and the lucidity and precision of scientific prose, and does not resort to imagery as a short cut, or as a way of evading the difficulty of formulating her perceptions in clear and objective terms. It is only after taking a firm foothold on objective and (if the concept can be applied to fiction) verifiable fact, that she makes the intuitive leap expressed in the poetic image.

Harold is not, of course, deficient in understanding. Here, quite late in the novel, he is described as giving Esther Lyon an account of the state of his mother's feelings:

But Harold Transome was more communicative about recent years that his mother was. He thought it well that Esther should know how the fortune of his family had been drained by law expenses, owing to suits mistakenly urged by her family; he spoke of his mother's lonely life and pinched circumstances, of her lack of comfort in her elder son, and of the habit she had consequently acquired of looking at the gloomy side of things. He hinted that she had been accustomed to dictate, and that, as he had left her when he was a boy, she had perhaps indulged the dream that he would come back a boy. She was still sore on the point of his politics. These things could not be helped, but, so far as he could, he wished to make the rest of her life as cheerful as possible. (352)

It would be hard to disagree with any part of this diagnosis. But Harold's understanding of his mother, though superficially accurate, is in the end an utter misunderstanding, for it leaves him able to believe that 'the rest of her life' can be made moderately 'cheerful'. He judges (as, within the limitations of our sympathetic imaginations, we must all judge) by reference to himself; so he believes that almost anything can be got over in time—that any disappointment, any resentment, any gloominess that Mrs Transome may feel can be forgotten at last if only things are made comfortable enough for her. And of course we must recognize the validity, within its limits, of Harold's account: if only Mrs Transome could have been persuaded to see herself and her troubles as clearly as this, she would no doubt conform herself to being comfortable. What is, however, awfully clear is that Mrs Transome's bitterness has a kind of life of its own; that it is beyond the reach of 'good sense'. One cannot argue a blight or a cancer out of existence, however unreasonable they may be; and when it was scientifically demonstrated that the wings of a bumble-bee were too small to bear a bee's weight, the bees went on flying as before.

If Harold's manner distresses the reader, it is because we have been led to feel for Mrs Transome so that we wish him capable, not only of understanding what makes her unhappy, but of making the great leap, the unreasoned and unreasonable surrender in tenderness and totally self-giving sympathy, which alone might have saved her. His failure to do so does not mark him as an unperceptive and mean-spirited man: it only marks him as a man not utterly unlike the rest of us.

It will be worth considering the nature and degree of Harold's delicacy in his relationship with Esther. He has, from the first, been impressed by her, and felt that she would look well in a luxurious setting; so, when it becomes clear that she has a strong claim to the Transome estate, he can hardly avoid the idea of marrying her.

He saw a mode of reconciling all difficulties which looked pleasanter to him the longer he looked at Esther. When she had been hardly a week in the house, he had made up his mind to marry her...To be deeply in love was a catastrophe not likely to happen to him; but he was readily amorous. No woman could make him miserable, but he was sensitive to the presence of women, and was kind to them; not with grimaces, like a man of mere gallantry, but beamingly, easily, like a man of genuine good-nature. And each day that he was near Esther, the solution of all difficulties by marriage became a more pleasing prospect. (352)

Is this a cynical device to retain possession of the estate? A careful consideration of this question will probably lead us outside the novel, to examine what may prove to be an inconsistency in our own standards, our criteria for judging a man's choice of a wife. May not our judgment depend, rather unreasonably, on how conscious Harold is of the train of motivation that is displayed here? In a roughly analogous situation in D. H. Lawrence's story *The Fox*, we are told that the young man 'seemed to calculate', and the word 'seemed' deters us from seeing him simply as calculating; besides, the story also contains a fox, which similarly *seems* to calculate. But George Eliot does not give us so much help here. If we imagine Harold thinking quite consciously of Esther as a means of solving the legal problems concerning the estate, we recoil from him in horror; but if he only feels these things intuitively and non-verbally, we may find his motivation quite acceptable. George Eliot often leaves a margin of un-certainty about the mental processes she describes: are they conscious or not? But if we find that this inhibits our response, the fault may be in our unreasonable tendency to allow a man's ignorance of his own motives to count in his favour.

Harold's courtship is, at any rate, assiduous and gallant. Esther, we are convinced, would see through any falsity in his behaviour; but the novel presents him throughout these scenes in an ironical light: he is shown as an accomplished, rather than as a sincere, lover.

Now consider how he speaks to Esther after he has discovered the secret of his birth.

'My feelings drag me another way. I need not tell you that your regard has become very important to me—that if our mutual position had been different —that, in short, you must have seen—if it had not seemed to be a matter of worldly interest, I should have told you plainly already that I loved you, and that my happiness could be complete only if you would consent to marry me.'

Esther felt her heart beginning to beat painfully. Harold's voice and words moved her so much that her own task seemed more difficult than she had before imagined. It seemed as if the silence, unbroken by anything but the clicking of the fire, had been long, before Harold turned round towards her again and said—

'But today I have heard something that affects my own position. I cannot tell you what it is. There is no need. It is not any culpability of my own. But I have not just the same unsullied name and fame in the eyes of the world around us, as I believed that I had when I allowed myself to entertain that wish about you. You are very young, entering on a fresh life with bright prospects—you are worthy of everything that is best. I may be too vain in thinking it was at all necessary; but I take this precaution against myself. I shut myself out from the chance of trying, after today, to induce you to accept anything which others may regard as specked and stained by any obloquy, however slight.'   (428)

Perhaps this shows that Harold has become a better man under the influence of his love for Esther; or perhaps he has been all along capable of generous feelings. This is one of the puzzles about him that make him, as a person in the novel, not inconsistent but entirely human. But in either case, he *is* capable of a generous response—and if he has failed to respond to his mother's emotional need it is not necessary or appropriate to attribute to him a grossness, a moral insensibility, inherited from Jermyn.

In other words, Mrs Transome's disappointment in her son is not a consequence of her having sinned at his begetting, but is perhaps a consequence of the more common human predicament of being a mother. Mrs Transome has been described (by F. R. Leavis in *The Great Tradition*) as 'a study in Nemesis': I think this places a misleading emphasis on an aspect of her sorrow that the novel does not make crucial. Nemesis is, in Greek tragedy, the retribution that falls on those who have undue good fortune, on those who are proud and over-confident, and on those who have committed singularly horrible crimes. The concept is present, for example, in the last speech of Oedipus in Sophocles' *Oedipus Rex*. I do not find it operating significantly in *Felix Holt*. Here is a passage where we might argue that the idea must be present—Mrs Transome and Matthew Jermyn are discussing the consequences of Harold's return home; Harold does not know that Jermyn is his father.

In this position, with a great dread hanging over her, which Jermyn knew, and ought to have felt that he had caused her, she was inclined to lash him with indignation, to scorch him with the words that were just the fit names for his doings—inclined all the more when he spoke with an insolent blandness, ignoring all that was truly in her heart. But no sooner did the words 'You have brought it on me' rise within her than she heard within also the retort, 'You brought it on yourself.' Nor for all the world beside could she bear to hear that retort uttered from without. What did she do? With strange sequence to all that rapid tumult, after a few moments' silence she said, in a gentle and almost tremulous voice—

'Let me take your arm.'   (107)

In her need to avoid a bitter confrontation between her son and his father, the masterful woman is reduced to pleading with her former lover; her unexpectedly taking Jermyn's arm reveals, more delicately and precisely than any 'flashback' could, the contrast between a past tenderness and a present indifference. But in essence it could all have happened—no less pathetically— if Jermyn had been her husband. The only element that is added by their sinful relationship over thirty years earlier is the danger that the truth may be revealed by Jermyn in anger; and the moment when that happens turns out to be a singularly unimpressive scene of unsuccessful melodrama (with a mirror too conveniently placed, so that Harold may have an opportunity of matching his face with Jermyn's). This would be a climax in the novel if Mrs Transome's case had been conceived as a study in Nemesis; instead, it is an absurd irrelevance.

What Mrs Transome endures is less extraordinary, and more centrally human, than 'Nemesis' suggests. She suffers the sorrow of being the mother of a son in whom she has put all her hopes of a happiness that he cannot begin to give her—a happiness that she may by now be incapable of experiencing; and she suffers the indifference and insolence of a man to whom she once gave (did she?) her love. Her pride, suppressed, turns gradually to a passive bitterness. She says to Esther,

'My dear, I shall make this house dull for you. You sit with me like embodied patience. I am unendurable; I am getting into a melancholy dotage. A fidgety old woman like me is as unpleasant to see as a rook with its wing broken. Don't mind me, my dear. Run away from me without ceremony. Every one else does, you see. I am part of the old furniture with new drapery.'

(399)

The portrayal of Mrs Transome is the most fully creative part of the novel, and by far the most moving. If I hesitate to call it *tragic*, it is because I think tragedy requires in the protagonist a richer imaginative awareness of what is happening to him; Mrs Transome's response to what she endures is perhaps too

static, too passive, to be called fully tragic. But the fact remains
that there is a dignity in her suffering—a dignity that George
Eliot honours with a significant omission; she never has Felix
Holt confront Mrs Transome. He could hardly exist—his
rhetoric could not survive—in her presence. For all her intellectual and moral mediocrity, she is a commanding presence in the
novel, compelling the reader's respect and sympathy even while
she loses hope of exercising authority, and making nonsense of
Felix's dogmatic assertion that

'One sort of fine-ladyism is as good as another.' (65)

6

'MIDDLEMARCH'

It may be useful to take our bearings on a stanza of Gray's
Elegy Written in a Country Churchyard (1750):

> Full many a gem of purest ray serene
> The dark unfathom'd caves of ocean bear:
> Full many a flower is born to blush unseen
> And waste its sweetness on the desert air.

The thousands of girls—not all of them living in rural areas—
who have underlined that stanza when they read it in some
anthology were not showing how deeply they were impressed by
the general truth of what it says; they were thinking of its special
(perhaps unique) applicability to themselves. They may have
said, 'How true!'; but they meant, 'Ah, how well that describes
my fate!'

George Eliot's treatment of Dorothea in *Middlemarch* has
been suspected of offering a similar temptation to the reader, and
of betraying a similar self-indulgence in the writer.[1] The 'Prelude'
to the novel must arouse such a suspicion.

That Spanish woman who lived three hundred years ago was certainly not the
last of her kind. Many Theresas have been born who found for themselves no
epic life wherein there was a constant unfolding of far-resonant action;
perhaps only a life of mistakes, the offspring of a certain spiritual grandeur
ill-matched with the meanness of opportunity; perhaps a tragic failure which
found no sacred poet and sank unwept into oblivion. With dim lights and
tangled circumstance they tried to shape their thought and deed in noble
agreement; but after all, to common eyes their struggles seemed mere
inconsistency and formlessness; for these later-born Theresas were helped
by no coherent social faith and order which could perform the function of
knowledge for the ardently willing soul. Their ardour alternated between a
vague ideal and a common yearning of womanhood; so that the one was
disapproved as extravagance, and the other condemned as a lapse.

(vol. I, xiii)

[1] See, in F. R. Leavis's illuminating account of the novel in *The Great
Tradition*, p. 75.

The dangerous tendency is certainly there, and it must be admitted that George Eliot yields to it—the tendency to slip into an emotional state that is too personal, too facile, too near to self-pity. If the novel fulfils the promise suggested by the 'Prelude', we can expect a sickly feast.

But fortunately the novel is not what the 'Prelude' suggests. Dorothea's superior sensibility, which in the 'Prelude' George Eliot seems to offer for our admiration, is perfectly dealt with in Chapter VII—

'No; but music of that sort I should enjoy', said Dorothea. 'When we were coming home from Lausanne my uncle took us to hear the great organ at Freiberg, and it made me sob.'

'That kind of thing is not healthy, my dear', said Mr. Brooke.

(I, 54)

Thomas Hardy admired the poem from which I have quoted; he took the title of one of his novels, *Far From the Madding Crowd*, from it. His novels too often do indulge this common inclination to see oneself as potentially great and obstructed by unfavourable circumstances. The purity of Tess of the Durbervilles, the intellectual capacity of Jude the Obscure, not only fail to find scope for their proper expression, but positively serve as magnets to attract misfortune. Anybody who is greater than the average, the common, or the mean, is the plaything of an ironical fate as all mankind is in Hardy's novels, but is also the victim of a resentful society, conditioned to destroy any rare exceptions among its members with all the righteous anger that mediocrity feels against the outstanding individual.

Middlemarch, too, deals with the relationship between the individual and society (as most novels do). But what we have seen of Mr Brooke's contribution to the sum of human wisdom is enough to suggest that mediocrity in her novels is not simply an object of hatred. Brooke, more than anyone else in the novel, stands for unfailing mediocrity, yet even he has a true word to say on occasion—and it comes with all the more startling force *because* it comes from him. Later we shall notice other indications that the mediocre small-town society in which Dorothea lives is not presented merely as an obstructive mass of upholders of useless convention, against which the rare individual must struggle hopelessly to be defeated in the end: it is, rather, the community that preserves (however limited and even stupid its members may be) an inherited wisdom about the human condition. This certainly resists the aspirations of the exceptional individual, but the resistance is necessary—it is the medium in which the individual lives, and shapes his destiny.

The parish of Tipton is not created by George Eliot to show how an unfavourable environment restricts the fine aspirations of her heroine. It is not because she cannot find anyone better that she marries Casaubon; in him, in Tipton, she finds and immediately recognizes the destiny she wants (or thinks she wants). The novel does not suggest that she would have chosen differently if she had had all London and Paris to choose from.

Whatever she may have thought when she was writing the 'Prelude', George Eliot knew well enough that what distinguishes the great is their ability to make the fullest use of even the most unpromising circumstances, and that a person who blames his environment for his failure to achieve anything is more likely to be making excuses than giving explanations. Her knowledge, which must have been based partly on her own experience of small-town life and of adverse circumstances against which she created her own life, is effective in the novel; it guides her imagination when she begins to see, in detail, step by step, what effect such an environment would really have on such a woman as Dorothea, and what is involved in being such a woman. Her remarks about St Theresa are a product of ideas about her, not of writing a novel about her; and George Eliot's intelligence, in spite of the intellectual power of her essays and reviews, is at its finest only when she writes as a novelist.

Another way of putting it would be to say that in reading the 'Prelude' we may agree or disagree with the ideas George Eliot expresses; but in reading the novel it would be as absurd to disagree with the events presented in it as to disagree with last month's rain. For there she is giving us not ideas but experiences; and they are created by her responsible imagination, which presents the world as it is and not as she would like it to be.

So although George Eliot can talk in general terms about 'a St. Theresa, foundress of nothing', it is a different matter when she sets out to create, with perfect honesty, a person in the novel— a person, not a generalization. And what she creates is not what the 'Prelude' seems to promise. Unusually intense spiritual aspirations in a real person have a limiting aspect.

> Her mind was theoretic, and yearned by its nature after some lofty conception of the world which might frankly include the parish of Tipton and her own rule of conduct there; she was enamoured of intensity and greatness, and rash in embracing whatever seemed to her to have those aspects; likely to seek martyrdom, to make retractations, and then to incur martyrdom after all in a quarter where she had not sought it. Certainly such elements in the character of a marriageable girl tended to interfere with her lot, and hinder it from being decided according to custom, by good looks, vanity, and merely canine affection. With all this, she, the elder of the sisters, was not yet twenty, and they had both been educated, since they were about twelve years old and had lost their parents, on plans at once narrow and promiscuous, first in an English family and afterwards in a Swiss family at Lausanne, their bachelor uncle and guardian trying in this way to remedy the disadvantages of their orphaned condition. (I, 2)

George Eliot cannot, in all honesty, offer us 'a St. Theresa, foundress of nothing'. To see the novelist's honesty triumphant so early in the novel promises well for the rest of it.

This is the special value of the novelist's imagination: that it can lead the writer to express more truth, more knowledge about the world as it really is, than any form of factual statement. In the play of *Sir Thomas More*, partly by Shakespeare, More addresses the London apprentices who are riotously demanding the expulsion of foreigners from the city:

> Imagine that you see the wretched strangers,
> Their babies at their backs, with their poor luggage,
> Plodding to the ports and coasts for transportation...

It is one thing to theorize about the effect of the foreigners on the local economy: it is another to 'imagine that you see the wretched strangers'. It is the special job of the writer of fiction to imagine that he sees.

George Eliot imagines Dorothea with characteristic thoroughness.

She was open, ardent, and not in the least self-admiring; indeed, it was pretty to see how her imagination adorned her sister Celia with attractions altogether superior to her own, and if any gentleman appeared to come to the Grange from some other motive than that of seeing Mr. Brooke, she concluded that he must be in love with Celia: Sir James Chettam, for example, whom she constantly considered from Celia's point of view, inwardly debating whether it would be good for Celia to accept him. That he should be regarded as a suitor to herself would have seemed to her a ridiculous irrelevance. Dorothea, with all her eagerness to know the truths of life, retained very childlike ideas about marriage. She felt sure that she would have accepted the judicious Hooker, if she had been born in time to save him from that wretched mistake he made in matrimony; or John Milton when his blindness had come on; or any of the other great men whose odd habits it would have been glorious piety to endure; but an amiable handsome baronet, who said 'Exactly' to her remarks even when she expressed uncertainty,—how could he affect her as a lover? The really delightful marriage must be that where your husband was a sort of father, and could teach you even Hebrew, if you wished it.

(I, 4)

There is both affectionate admiration and gentle mockery here. The mockery is explicit in the statement that Dorothea 'retained very childlike ideas about marriage' but it does not invite the reader to feel superior to her. 'Childlike', unlike 'childish', is generally a word of praise, suggesting innocence rather than folly; and there is both admiration for Dorothea's confidence in her ability to sustain an extraordinary destiny, and pity for her ignorance of the reality of endurance, in 'any of the other great men whose odd habits it would have been glorious piety to endure'. The short account of Sir James Chettam here is enough to make the question '—how could he affect her as a lover?' seem as if George Eliot is asking the question herself, as well as reporting it, so to speak, as Dorothea's. But the last sentence of the paragraph, with its naïve confusion of the roles of husband, father and teacher and its comic suggestion that learning Hebrew is the climax of a 'really delightful marriage', arranges Dorothea's view of the matter in such a way as to emphasize its absurdity.

But it is not absurd that Dorothea should wish to marry an educated and intelligent man; and even her wish that her husband might be rather like a father may seem less ridiculous when we see what an unsatisfactory substitute for a wise and learned father Dorothea has had from the age of twelve—Mr Brooke, her uncle:

'Young ladies don't understand political economy, you know', said Mr. Brooke, smiling towards Mr. Casaubon. 'I remember when we were all reading Adam Smith. *There* is a book, now. I took in all the new ideas at one time—human perfectibility, now. But some say, history moves in circles; and that may be very well argued; I have argued it myself. The fact is, human reason may carry you a little too far—over the hedge, in fact. It carried me a good way at one time; but I saw it would not do. I pulled up; I pulled up in time. But not too hard. I have always been in favour of a little theory: we must have Thought; else we shall be landed back in the dark ages. But talking of books, there is Southey's "Peninsular War." I am reading that of a morning. You know Southey?'   (I, 10)

The effects of such an upbringing are evident both in Dorothea's earnest wish for some systematic guidance in her studies, and in the lack of training in habits of coherent logical thinking that is revealed in her own reported thoughts—here, for example, where she is clearly the niece of Mr Brooke:

Perhaps even Hebrew might be necessary—at least the alphabet and a few roots—in order to arrive at the core of things, and judge soundly on the social duties of the Christian.   (I, 52)

But if we continue reading that paragraph, we find a complexity of ironies that are by no means all directed against Dorothea's naïveté:

And she had not reached that point of renunciation at which she would have been satisfied with having a wise husband; she wished, poor child, to be wise herself. Miss Brooke was certainly very naïve with all her alleged cleverness. Celia, whose mind had never been thought too powerful, saw the emptiness of other people's pretensions much more readily. To have in general but little feeling, seems to be the only security against feeling too much on any particular occasion.   (I, 52)

That 'renunciation' is not offered unironically as an ideal; and it is the voice of social convention that is parodied in 'she wished, *poor child*, to be wise herself' and in calling her naïve in the next sentence. Celia's solution, in the final sentence, is not one that the novelist advocates or acts upon, though it does usefully describe the risk, and probable cost, of feeling deeply.

This is characteristic of the voice of the novelist in *Middlemarch*. The ironies shift from sentence to sentence, phrase to phrase, demanding an alertness on the part of the reader to answer the agility of the writer's mind. Not that she always, even in this novel, maintains such a fine control and poise of tone; she loses it, for example, here—

Let any lady who is inclined to be hard on Mrs. Cadwallader inquire into the comprehensiveness of her own beautiful views, and be quite sure that they afford accommodation for all the lives which have the honour to coexist with hers.   (I, 49)

To say this, George Eliot must have lost faith for the moment in the novel's ability to communicate such suggestions as these, and far more subtle ones, without making them explicitly. The statement is sound enough in itself, but it did not need to be made; and the sarcasm of 'which have the honour...' is embarrassing. Compare it with another sentence that occurs very soon after it:

From the first arrival of the young ladies in Tipton she had prearranged Dorothea's marriage with Sir James, and if it had taken place would have been quite sure that it was her doing: that it should not take place after she had preconceived it, caused her an irritation which every thinker will sympathise with.   (I, 49)

This far more effectively invites the reader to recognize similar propensities in himself, without explicitly addressing him. The description of motive, here as often in the novel, has to be completed by the reader's introspection; we have to participate in order to understand it.

The ways in which George Eliot writes about the people she creates in the novel suggest something of the complexity that is required in thinking about real people; in that sense the novel is a moral example. The various shifts of tone that produce, in *Middlemarch*, such a delicate interplay of irony and sympathy express the simultaneous presence of the detachment that makes judgment possible, and the attachment that finds people worth judging. Without this detachment, judgment would be impossible, and sympathy and understanding would lead to the conviction that 'to know all is to forgive all'—an indiscriminate indulgence. Without the author's attachment to people, judgment would be a futile academic exercise. I do not mean that George Eliot was, or that the reader becomes, attached to Dorothea, Lydgate, and other imagined characters in the novel; this would be a somewhat absurd sentimentality, because these 'people' do not exist. But the ways in which George Eliot presents them, and the corresponding ways in which we apprehend them, are closely related to habits of concern and care for actual people.

What George Eliot never shows in this novel is indifference to people (though we have noticed a suspicion of it in some parts of *Adam Bede*).

There are three conditions which often look alike
Yet differ completely, flourish in the same hedgerow:
Attachment to self and to things and to persons, detachment
From self and from things and from persons; and, growing between them, indifference
Which resembles the others as death resembles life,
Being between two lives—unflowering, between
The live and the dead nettle...   (T. S. Eliot, *Little Gidding* III)

The attachment and detachment that I have been calling attention to are, in the first place, qualities of George Eliot's mind, habits of thought and feeling about other people, which give her two ways of looking at them; and, rather as our two eyes, giving us two slightly different images of things we see, give us our sense of depth and distance, so the two simultaneous ways of regarding people and their actions give George Eliot's vision of life and relationships a depth, a three-dimensional quality. We have noticed its effect on the quality of her descriptive prose, which is saved from becoming theoretical by shifting its ground even within one sentence—sometimes mocking one person's views from the point of view of others, sometimes revealing the deficiencies in the others and recognizing the value of the odd one, sometimes taking the reader by surprise and disturbing *his* complacency by showing what is admirable in what she has seemed to encourage him to mock.

In *Middlemarch* this double vision has a special importance because a central theme of the novel is the complexity of the relationships between the exceptional individual and the ordinary society in which he lives. We shall return to this later; for the present I shall only suggest that the novel establishes its positive values not by vindicating Dorothea against the belittling society in which she lives, nor by showing that this society was right after all and cutting Dorothea's eccentric aspirations down to size, but by claiming recognition for the opposing truths of both views, so that a more comprehensive and balanced truth emerges from their interaction. So it is wrong to discount, as F. R. Leavis does, Brooke's diagnosis of Dorothea's exaltations ("'That kind of thing is not healthy, my dear'") on the grounds that it comes from 'the fatuous Mr. Brooke, a figure consistently presented for our ironic contemplation'. For this is to ignore the choric significance, in the novel, of characters not wise in themselves but commanding, in the aggregate, something of a traditional and 'social' wisdom that has to be taken seriously.

Marrying Casaubon is Dorothea's most significant act in the first half of the novel, and we inevitably judge her partly by this act of free choice. What kind of man does she choose? Part of the answer comes from people whose judgments we have little cause to trust as individuals; people who have their own interests in the matter, more or less directly; people who are not distinguished for the coolness, delicacy and precision of their objective judgments. Sir James Chettam's reaction to the news of Dorothea's engagement is presented in involuntary actions as well as words:

'Very well. She is engaged to be married.' Mrs. Cadwallader paused a few moments, observing the deeply-hurt expression in her friend's face, which he was trying to conceal by a nervous smile, while he whipped his boot; but she soon added, 'Engaged to Casaubon.'

Sir James let his whip fall and stooped to pick it up. Perhaps his face had never before gathered so much concentrated disgust as when he turned to Mrs. Cadwallader and repeated, 'Casaubon?'

'Even so. You know my errand now.'

'Good God! It is horrible! He is no better than a mummy!' (The point of view has to be allowed for, as that of a blooming and disappointed rival.)

'She says, he is a great soul.—A great bladder for dried peas to rattle in!' said Mrs. Cadwallader.

'What business has an old bachelor like that to marry?' said Sir James. 'He has one foot in the grave.'

'He means to draw it out again, I suppose.'

'Brooke ought not to allow it: he should insist on its being put off till she is of age. She would think better of it then. What is a guardian for?' (I, 47)

The novelist's hasty intervention is partly ironical in its effect—it modifies, but does not negate, Chettam's view. And although we can hardly agree that Brooke ought to forbid the marriage, Chettam's honest indignation compels some response in the reader. Mrs Cadwallader has already expressed her feelings about Casaubon in conversation with Celia:

'As to his blood, I suppose the family quarterings are three cuttle-fish sable, and a commentator rampant.' (I, 45)

She appears to be talking about Casaubon's lack of aristocratic descent—a characteristic preoccupation of hers; but the phrase 'cuttle-fish sable' seems to comment on his lack of 'blood' in another sense—his lack of warmth and vigour. He has, she implies, neither the blue blood of nobility, nor the red blood of virility: ink flows in his veins instead. Later, to her husband, she speaks of Dorothea's marriage as a perverse choice of archaic monastic austerity.

'I throw her over: there was a chance, if she had married Sir James, of her becoming a sane, sensible woman. He would never have contradicted her, and when a woman is not contradicted, she has no motive for obstinacy in her absurdities. But now I wish her joy of her hair shirt.' (I, 49)

And Sir James's remark to Mr Cadwallader is, in its own terms, unanswerable:

'But look at Casaubon', said Sir James, indignantly. 'He must be fifty, and I don't believe he could ever have been much more than the shadow of a man. Look at his legs!' (I, 56)

So we have this choric commentary on Casaubon to set against Dorothea's impression of him, and it is not negligible—it does not merely suggest how little the world understands him.

There is another way in which Casaubon is presented to us, a way that defines with remarkable precision what we may call the quality of a life—not in terms of moral excellence and defects, nor in terms of the more readily recognizable manly virtues, but giving an immediate sense of the kind of person he is. The descriptions of his and Chettam's houses at the beginning of Chapter XI are not merely descriptions of houses, setting the scene for subsequent action; George Eliot's interest is not primarily architectural. The descriptions throw light on the owners of the houses in two ways—both in that one can, quite rationally, deduce something about a man from the house he chooses to inhabit, and by direct symbolic comment: it is not only Casaubon's house but his soul that is here described, and the prospects of life from the windows of his mind, with its areas of spacious order and classical clarity and its areas of sunlessness.

On a grey but dry November morning Dorothea drove to Lowick in company with her uncle and Celia. Mr. Casaubon's home was the manor-house. Close by, visible from some parts of the garden, was the little church, with the old parsonage opposite. In the beginning of his career, Mr. Casaubon had only held the living, but the death of his brother had put him in possession of the manor also. It had a small park, with a fine old oak here and there, and an avenue of limes towards the south-west front, with a sunk fence between park and pleasure-ground, so that from the drawing-room windows the glance swept uninterruptedly along a slope of greensward till the limes ended in a level of corn and pastures, which often seemed to melt into a lake under the setting sun. This was the happy side of the house, for the south and east looked rather melancholy even under the brightest morning. The grounds here were more confined, the flower-beds showed no very careful tendance, and large clumps of trees, chiefly of sombre yews, had risen high, not ten yards from the windows. The building, of greenish stone, was in the old English style, not ugly, but small-windowed and melancholy-looking: the sort of house that must have children, many flowers, open windows, and little vistas of bright things, to make it seem a joyous home. In this latter end of autumn, with a sparse remnant of yellow leaves falling slowly athwart the dark evergreens in a stillness without sunshine, the house too had an air of autumnal decline, and Mr. Casaubon, when he presented himself, had no bloom that could be thrown into relief by that background.   (I, 60)

Casaubon is a scholar, but a scholar doomed to failure. Not because of the nature of his task: his projected *Key to All the Mythologies* can hardly seem absurd today, when we are accustomed to the presence in libraries of Frazer's *The Golden Bough*. But Casaubon's task is felt to be, as he sets about it, endless; his sight is already failing. He gains our admiration and pity here, even while we recognize the fruitlessness of his labours. George Eliot lets others comment on him, but the fact that all but Dorothea are against him is shown to be only partly justified; and it heightens the impression of Dorothea's lonely courage in believing in him. She may be right, and the devotion she offers strikes us as having the power, if anything has, of inducing in Casaubon the strength and firmness he needs if his work is to be completed. It is worth noticing that George Eliot makes very modest claims for Dorothea's judgment. The reader has sufficient opportunity to conclude that Dorothea is more intelligent—or at least more rational—as well as being more sensitive to possibilities of greatness than are Mr Brooke, Celia, Chettam and Mrs Cadwallader, and is thus quite likely to be more right than they are about an extraordinary person, but George Eliot does not explicitly make any such claim for her. She says only that Dorothea might, just by chance, have turned out to be right.

Because Miss Brooke was hasty in her trust, it is not therefore clear that Mr. Casaubon was unworthy of it. (I, 17)

The point, then, about the various comments on Casaubon by persons of limited understanding and imagination is not that by weight of numbers they counterbalance Dorothea's more sympathetic view—but that for all their various blindnesses they share in a view of Casaubon as scholar that can be called traditional; it is a view suggested in the epigraph to Chapter v.

'Hard students are commonly troubled with gowts, catarrhs, rheums, cachexia, bradypepsia, bad eyes, stone, and collick, crudities, oppilations, vertigo, winds, consumptions, and all such diseases as come by over-much sitting: they are most part lean, dry, ill-coloured...and all through immoderate pains and extraordinary studies. If you will not believe the truth of this, look upon great Tostatus and Thomas Aquinas' works; and tell me whether those men took pains.'— Burton's *Anatomy of Melancholy*, P.I.S.2.
(I, 33)

Such a traditional view can supply some of the deficiencies in the view of the exceptional individual who thinks freshly for himself, as J. S. Mill, in his essay on Jeremy Bentham, had pointed out— in terms that George Eliot seems to recall several times in *Middlemarch*:

Even the originality which can, and the courage which dares, think for itself, is not a more necessary part of the philosophical character than a thoughtful regard for previous thinkers, and for the collective mind of the human race. What has been the opinion of mankind, has been the opinion of persons of all tempers and dispositions, of all partialities and prepossessions, of all varieties in position, in education, in opportunities of observation and inquiry. No one inquirer is all this...Every circumstance which gives a character to the life of a human being, carries with it its peculiar biasses; its peculiar facilities for perceiving some things, and for missing or forgetting others. But, from points of view different from his, different things are perceptible; and none are more likely to have seen what he does not see, than those who do not see what he sees...The collective mind does not penetrate below the surface, but it sees all the surface; which profound thinkers, even by reason of their profundity, often fail to do: their intenser view of a thing in some of its aspects diverting the attention from others. (*Mill on Bentham and Coleridge*, ed. F. R. Leavis, Chatto & Windus 1967; pp. 59–60)

As Celia says to Dorothea,

'You always see what nobody else sees; it is impossible to satisfy you; yet you never see what is quite plain.' (I, 27)

It is the continual awareness both of what the individual sees and of what 'the collective mind' sees that gives the prose of *Middlemarch* its distinctive quality, and constantly implies judgments that are at the same time rigorous and sympathetic.

Casaubon's letter proposing marriage to Dorothea (Chapter V, vol. I, p. 33) is too long to quote, but it should be studied attentively. It is, as it says, 'the accurate statement of his feelings'; but always a statement, not an expression, of feelings. Its style may strike us as a parody of a pedantic love-letter: yet we cannot miss its complete seriousness, or the way in which it pays Dorothea the compliment of assuming her to be an intelligent adult accustomed to reading strenuous prose.

I am not, I trust, mistaken in the recognition of some deeper correspondence than that of date in the fact that a consciousness of need in my own life had arisen contemporaneously with the possibility of my becoming acquainted with you. (I, 33)

There is something horrifying in this way of writing to a young girl. Yet Dorothea is an uncommon young girl, as Casaubon explicitly recognizes—

Our conversations have, I think, made sufficiently clear to you the tenor of my life and purposes: a tenor unsuited, I am aware, to the commoner order of minds. (I, 33)

And it is because he is an uncommon man that he can recognize her; there is an affinity between them, that places them together against the unappreciative world, which lacks their standards of dedication and austerity. However we may mock Casaubon, we must also be humbled by his ability to assert without reservation that his life,

however short in the sequel, has no backward pages whereon, if you choose to turn them, you will find records such as might justly cause you either bitterness or shame. (I, 33)

But although we must, in justice to Casaubon, respect him and give him credit for being the first to recognize Dorothea's uniqueness, we cannot help noticing also—with pity for him as well as for her—how ineptly he responds to it. The strongest effect of his letter is to make us receptive to Celia's impression,

There was something funereal in the whole affair, and Mr. Casaubon seemed to be the officiating clergyman, about whom it would be indecent to make remarks. (I, 39)

What needs to be said about Dorothea's reply can best be suggested by quoting a comment that seems to me to be as far as possible from the truth. It is from Virginia Woolf's essay entitled 'George Eliot' in *The Common Reader*, and here she is making a contrast between George Eliot and Jane Austen:

She allows her heroines to talk too much. She has little verbal felicity. She lacks the unerring taste which chooses one sentence and compresses the heart of the scene within that. 'Whom are you going to dance with?' asked Mr. Knightley, at the Weston's ball. 'With you, if you will ask me', said Emma; and she has said enough. Mrs. Casaubon would have talked for an hour and we should have looked out of the window.

Here is Dorothea's letter in reply to Casaubon's proposal:

MY DEAR MR. CASAUBON,—I am very grateful to you for loving me, and thinking me worthy to be your wife. I can look forward to no better happiness than that which would be one with yours. If I said more, it would only be the same thing written out at greater length, for I cannot now dwell on any other thought than that I may be through life

Yours devotedly,
DOROTHEA BROOKE. (I, 35)

There is something magnificently absurd in Dorothea's choice of Casaubon. Here I want to mention one other way in which the absurdity is stressed: that is, by the implicit comment that echoes back, so to speak, from the description given later of what 'falling in love' means to Rosamond Vincy. This description turns out to be surprisingly applicable to Dorothea's apparently very different self-dedication to Casaubon; the fundamental diagnosis of the error of the choice is similar in the two cases.

And here was Mr. Lydgate suddenly corresponding to her ideal, being altogether foreign to Middlemarch, carrying a certain air of distinction congruous with good family, and possessing connections which offered vistas of that middle-class heaven, rank: a man of talent, also, whom it would be especially delightful to enslave: in fact, a man who had touched her nature quite newly, and brought a vivid interest into her life which was better than any fancied 'might-be' such as she was in the habit of opposing to the actual.

(I, 102)

The differences are plain: Dorothea's prospect of delight is in devoting herself to her husband rather than in enslaving him; and her 'heaven' is not rank but learning. But the radical similarity is also clear. I am not now thinking of the Romantic preference for exogamy, though that is significantly present in both, but of the preconceived ideal conceived in 'opposition to the actual': both girls have reacted against their homes by dreaming of somebody quite different whom they will marry, and their choice of a husband consequently becomes, not so much a selection from among various known realities, as a sense of recognizing the fulfilment of their day-dreams. Reading of Rosamond's view of Lydgate as a man made to her own specifications, we are reminded that Dorothea has found in Casaubon a close approximation to her notion of the judicious Hooker or the blind John Milton.

Our feeling about Dorothea's choice, then, is complex. But we must remember that such a statement is merely a convenient, short way of saying that the novelist, in her presentation of the imagined Dorothea, gives us a demonstration, an example, of moral complexity in human choices. And in so far as Dorothea is fully imagined, we respond to her choices and actions almost as if we were reading about a real person, so that the moral complexity exists in our own response and is not just displayed in the novel for us to look at. The distinction I am drawing attention to here may seem to be a hair-splitting one, but I think it is important: the novel is really about people—about, for example, us, and our friends; Dorothea and Casaubon are imaginary illustrations of the things George Eliot knew about people.

So we continually look outwards, from the novel, to see how the knowledge it transmits will affect our judgments of real people and their decisions. The novel implies generalizations. Here, for example, Dorothea's decision to marry Casaubon is shown in such a way as to draw attention, not to the wrongness of her choice, but to the inevitable incompleteness of every individual judgment on it. This must obviously tend to make our moral judgments in general more tentative, less dogmatic, than they would have been without the novel's lesson. Even the consequences of the decision do not provide a conclusive judgment on it; however unhappy Dorothea becomes as a result of marrying Casaubon, we cannot see Chettam's comment on the marriage as expressing a finer and surer response to her choice than Dorothea's own.

I spoke of the inevitable incompleteness of every individual judgment. But there is an exception. The novel itself achieves the completeness that no merely individual view can attain; George Eliot, as novelist, seems then to transcend the limitations of the individual judgment, and enables the reader to do so with her. She does so, and shows us how to do so, by *imagining* reactions different from our own merely personal ones, by recognizing fully the validity of responses that are different from our own.

Perhaps the point of this digression will now be clear. It is not what we think of Dorothea that matters (though, for brevity, I shall often be talking as if it were), but the training that the novel gives to our sympathy and imagination, as means of approaching judgments that are not limited by our personal prejudices and the circumstances in which we happen to be placed.

We have seen how Dorothea thinks of Casaubon as a kind of father and teacher, rather than as a husband, properly speaking. Of their relationship as husband and wife we have several ominous forewarnings, mostly in accounts of Casaubon's thoughts and feelings. Already in his letter of proposal we may have noticed with misgivings his offer of 'an affection hitherto unwasted', which, although it indicates his premarital chastity, suggests a rather simple notion of 'affection' as something that can be saved up until one is ready to release it—so that the less affection one has given, the more one will have accumulated. Later the image of the shallow stream, while it applies explicitly to the weakness of his emotions, implicitly suggests the ageing man's declining virility—

Hence he determined to abandon himself to the stream of feeling, and perhaps was surprised to find what an exceedingly shallow rill it was. As in droughty regions baptism by immersion could only be performed symbolically, so Mr. Casaubon found that sprinkling was the utmost approach to a plunge which his stream would afford him; and he concluded that the poet had much exaggerated the force of masculine passion.   (I, 51)

And we might find further cause for misgivings in Casaubon's wish that Dorothea's sister should accompany them on the wedding journey.

When we next see Dorothea, after her marriage, she is in Rome. We see her, in Chapter XIX, through the eyes of Will Ladislaw, whose attention is drawn to her by his friend, a German artist, among the sculptures in the Vatican.

Quickness was ready at the call, and the two figures passed lightly along by the Meleager towards the hall where the reclining Ariadne, then called the Cleopatra, lies in the marble voluptuousness of her beauty, the drapery folding around her with a petal-like ease and tenderness. They were just in time to see another figure standing against a pedestal near the reclining marble: a breathing blooming girl, whose form, not shamed by the Ariadne, was clad in Quakerish grey drapery; her long cloak, fastened at the neck, was thrown backward from her arms, and one beautiful ungloved hand pillowed her cheek, pushing somewhat backward the white beaver bonnet which made a sort of halo to her face around the simply braided dark-brown hair. She was not looking at the sculpture, probably not thinking of it: her large eyes were fixed dreamily on a streak of sunlight which fell across the floor.   (I, 165)

This is the first time George Eliot has invited us to look at Dorothea as an image of feminine beauty, a source of visual delight. In her provincial environment there has been nobody capable of responding, as Ladislaw and the German artist do, to the beauty of her form and movement, and the novelist has been too scrupulous to present to the reader a view that is not registered in the awareness of any person present at the time. Dorothea's physical beauty, unregarded by herself, obscured by familiarity

73

in the eyes of her neighbours and dimmed by excessive study in those her husband, seems not to have existed before; now the novel brings her to Rome, where the trained eye of the German artist and an environment that provides standards for comparison enable that beauty to be properly appreciated and—for the first time—fully to exist.

What Dorothea's beauty as 'a breathing blooming girl' makes us almost painfully aware of now is a dimension of her life that has been insufficiently taken into account before—particularly by Dorothea herself: a potential capacity for sensuous delight. Her body is so placed as to invite, and it bears, the most challenging comparison—'not shamed by the Ariadne'—and this suggests some relationship, strange and to be wondered about, between Dorothea and 'voluptuousness'. The German artist's first comment notes only a part of that relationship; he remarks on 'a fine bit of antithesis'. The reader may now recall impressions made, but not emphasized, earlier in the novel:

Riding was an indulgence which she allowed herself in spite of conscientious qualms; she felt that she enjoyed it in a pagan sensuous way, and always looked forward to renouncing it. (I, 4)

and Dorothea's delight in the jewels which she also despises.

The German artist goes on:

'But she should be dressed as a nun; I think she looks almost what you call a Quaker. I would dress her as a nun in my picture. However, she is married; I saw her wedding-ring on that wonderful left hand, otherwise I should have thought the sallow *Geistlicher* was her father.' (I, 166)

Geistlicher means, simply, a clergyman; but the word has a resonance—at least for the English ear—of unphysicality, almost of gruesome separation from the flesh.

The detachment with which the painter talks about her, in purely visual terms (or almost purely—for he does want her to represent, in a painting, an abstract idea), makes it possible for the incongruity of her position to be presented to us without the emotional involvement that would be inevitable if we were looking directly at her. Her earlier thought that a husband should be a sort of father reappears in a different light now she is married, in 'otherwise I should have thought the sallow *Geistlicher* was her father'; and the absurdity of the match, visually regarded, is exploited by Naumann's teasing Ladislaw by referring to Dorothea as his great-aunt.

The direct look, with the emotional involvement (which is not, however, of a distorting kind) comes at the beginning of Chapter XX.

Two hours later, Dorothea was seated in an inner room or boudoir of a handsome apartment in the Via Sistina.

I am sorry to add that she was sobbing bitterly, with such abandonment to this relief of an oppressed heart as a woman habitually controlled by pride on her own account and thoughtfulness for others will sometimes allow herself when she feels securely alone. And Mr. Casaubon was certain to remain away for some time at the Vatican. (I, 169)

Casaubon's lack of vital response, his inability (or habitual refusal, which comes to the same thing) to respond spontaneously, is evident at once in his way of talking about art. At the same time, Dorothea's relationship with him is suggested.

'Should you like to go to the Farnesina, Dorothea? It contains celebrated frescoes designed or painted by Raphael, which most persons think it worth while to visit.'

'But do you care about them?' was always Dorothea's question.

'They are, I believe, highly esteemed. Some of them represent the fable of Cupid and Psyche, which is probably the romantic invention of a literary period, and cannot, I think, be reckoned as a genuine mythical product. But if you like these wall-paintings we can easily drive thither; and you will then, I think, have seen the chief works of Raphael, any of which it were a pity to omit in a visit to Rome. He is the painter who has been held to combine the most complete grace of form with sublimity of expression. Such at least I have gathered to be the opinion of cognoscenti.'

This kind of answer given in a measured official tone, as of a clergyman reading according to the rubric, did not help to justify the glories of the Eternal City, or to give her the hope that if she knew more about them the world would be joyously illuminated for her. There is hardly any contact more depressing to a young ardent creature than that of a mind in which years full of knowledge seem to have issued in a blank absence of interest or sympathy. (I, 173)

The chapter is a particularly rich one, and will repay the closest study. George Eliot makes the necessary comment: there seems nothing to add. The commentator's difficulty is to find parts of the chapter that he can bear not to quote. The next paragraph, in which Casaubon's scholarly labours are described with pity, ends with the terrible epigram—

With his taper stuck before him he forgot the absence of windows, and in bitter manuscript remarks on other men's notions about the solar deities, he had become indifferent to the sunlight. (I, 174)

The next is a moving description of the lack, in Casaubon's response to Dorothea, of that tenderness that expresses itself through touch. She, we are told, 'had ardour enough...to have kissed Mr Casaubon's coat-sleeve, or to have caressed his shoe-latchet'—but he would have 'regarded these manifestations as rather crude and startling'.

Having made his clerical toilette with due care in the morning, he was prepared only for those amenities of life which were suited to the well-adjusted stiff cravat of the period, and to a mind weighted with unpublished matter. (I, 175)

But this novel does not allow us the easy luxury of unmixed pity; the habit of mind that favours indulgence in an unresisted, unchecked flow of feeling 'for' somebody regarded as a wholly innocent victim of circumstances is perhaps the same habit that permits the uncritical enjoyment of self-pity. Even while the misery of Dorothea's touch-starvation is most vividly experienced, we are not allowed to forget that Casaubon too is pitiable, nor that Dorothea has incurred responsibilities towards him by marrying him. The very weaknesses that made him repellent earlier are pitiable now; it is not appropriate for Dorothea to reproach him now as it would have been appropriate for her to regard his scholarship critically before deciding to marry him.

'And all your notes', said Dorothea, whose heart had already burned within her on this subject, so that now she could not help speaking with her tongue. 'All those rows of volumes—will you not now do what you used to speak of? —will you not make up your mind what part of them you will use, and begin to write the book which will make your vast knowledge useful to the world? I will write to your dictation, or I will copy and extract what you tell me: I can be of no other use.' Dorothea, in a most unaccountable, darkly-feminine manner, ended with a slight sob and eyes full of tears. (I, 176)

In the failure of the relationship, the failure of sympathetic communication, Dorothea has a share: this speech shows how little she enters into his feelings, his doubts and fears. She is aware only of *her* feelings towards him; and however self-sacrificing those feelings are, they are not fully, sympathetically, responsive to him. They have been based on admiration for Casaubon, a sentiment that maintains separateness, rather than on sympathy, which unites.

The novel does not make us entirely dependent on Dorothea's view of Casaubon's studies. We have also his own utterances, and the novelist's account of his self-doubting fears. Our own judgment is thus not limited, as Dorothea's is, to deploring the lack of results in a form ready for publication. We are given room to reflect that it is usually a delicate question, whether and when and how one should urge a scholar to stop accumulating material and start organizing it; a delicate task to estimate how far that organization has already proceeded in his mind. In such a vast undertaking as Casaubon's, premature insistence on a set of chapter-headings can reduce to total collapse the structure that may have been taking shape in his mind. It will be noticed that I am again looking outside the novel, looking for possible relations between Casaubon's situation and others that one has encountered: this is what the novel continually obliges one to do—one understands it by looking beyond its immediate local meaning. One thinks how often a supervisor of graduate studies, or a publisher, is inclined to say—as many ruthlessly do say—something like

'All those rows of volumes...will you not make up your mind what part of them you will use, and begin to write the book which will make your vast knowledge useful to the world?'

There are circumstances in which such a plea is necessary, and relationships in which it is appropriate. It can be an expression of care and concern for the writer who is in danger of excessive accumulation of uncharted knowledge. But it is not what Casaubon needs at this moment, and Dorothea has not as a wife created the relationship in which she might say it without danger. Casaubon's reply must be taken seriously, although it is made in a manner that makes one shudder. The manner is explained, though not excused, by the fact that Casaubon has rehearsed it in answer to imaginary hostile criticism; the fact that Dorothea's plea triggers it off shows how closely her words have approximated to those of

Casaubon's imagined critic, as well as Casaubon's pressing need to defend himself:

> 'My love,' he said, with irritation reined in by propriety, 'you may rely upon me for knowing the times and seasons, adapted to the different stages of a work which is not to be measured by the facile conjectures of ignorant onlookers. It had been easy for me to gain a temporary effect by a mirage of baseless opinion; but it is ever the trial of the scrupulous explorer to be saluted with the impatient scorn of chatterers who attempt only the smallest achievements, being indeed equipped for no other. And it were well if all such could be admonished to discriminate judgments of which the true subject-matter lies entirely beyond their reach, from those of which the elements may be compassed by a narrow and superficial survey.'
>
> (I, 177)

George Eliot comments, presenting Casaubon's view,

> Dorothea was not only his wife: she was a personification of that shallow world which surrounds the ill-appreciated or desponding author.
>
> (I, 177)

Our sympathies can hardly rest even momentarily with Casaubon in this exchange. But he has some justification, which we are not in a position to evaluate conclusively—for we, like Dorothea, are not likely to be competent judges of his scholarship.

Dorothea's weakening confidence in her husband's mastery of his chosen field of study is evident in her response to Ladislaw's comment on his 'devoted labour':

> 'It is a pity that it should be thrown away, as so much English scholarship is, for want of knowing what is being done by the rest of the world. If Mr. Casaubon read German he would save himself a great deal of trouble.'
> 'I do not understand you', said Dorothea, startled and anxious.
>
> (I, 183)

It is not on the basis of any specialized knowledge that Dorothea has begun to distrust her husband's judgment and competence in his own work, and shows herself predisposed to accept Ladislaw's assessment (which is itself very insecurely based). But Dorothea has other reasons, perhaps more compelling ones: she is married to him, and now has a knowledge that she did not have before of the weakness of the flame of life in Casaubon: his inadequacy as a man. His inadequacy as a scholar is a part of that. What the novel shows us in these chapters is Dorothea's experience of marriage with Casaubon; and although George Eliot observes the reticences of her time, there is no doubt that the experience is fully imagined at every level. The novelist does not tell us about the intimacies of their life as husband and wife—but how well one *knows*!

It is clear that Dorothea has begun to lose confidence in her husband's work before Ladislaw hints to her that he is not adequately equipped for it. It is too easy for us, knowing the sequel, to suppose her loss of faith justified by his ultimate failure; but we should not ignore the possibility that her loss of faith in him contributes to that failure. At least she does not find the way, if there is a way, of helping him to succeed.

The twenty-first chapter of *Middlemarch* ends with this paragraph:

We are all of us born in moral stupidity, taking the world as an udder to feed our supreme selves: Dorothea had early begun to emerge from that stupidity, but yet it had been easier to her to imagine how she would devote herself to Mr. Casaubon, and become wise and strong in his strength and wisdom, than to conceive with that distinctness which is no longer reflection but feeling—an idea wrought back to the directness of sense, like the solidity of objects—that he had an equivalent centre of self, whence the lights and shadows must always fall with a certain difference. (1, 186)

The paragraph is one of the great focal points of George Eliot's art, expanding—or exploding—into generalization from the particular consideration of Dorothea. In fact it would not be very misleading to think of the entire creation of Dorothea's marriage as the means by which the novelist gives the reader the experience he needs in order to grasp the knowledge that she offers here. There are, of course, different modes of 'knowledge'. There are many things we know theoretically—that the earth travels round the sun, that millions of people as real as ourselves live in distant parts of the world, or that a molecule of water is made up of one atom of oxygen and two of hydrogen—without effectively believing them; perhaps there is no room in our minds for full imaginative experience of all we know. George Eliot is deeply concerned with the difference between merely knowing something as a fact, and knowing something as a felt experience that influences one's feelings and conduct.

The distinction is a hard one to explain, and the novelist strains words to their limit in the attempt. For the reader has to be made to understand not only intellectually but 'with that distinctness which is no longer reflection but feeling—an idea wrought back to the directness of sense, like the solidity of objects'. That, of course, is precisely what the first part of the opening sentence enacts; the statement is first made in abstract terms, and then embodied in the solidity of the young animal at the udder—an image that not only illustrates the statement but also suggests an explanation for the fact. The baby at the breast, not yet very different from other young animals, sees the world in terms of its response to its own needs; only gradually do we become aware of the independent, autonomous reality of other people. Earlier writers could have used the doctrine of original sin to make a similar observation; George Eliot prefers to hint at a biological account. Again, in the final sentence the novelist turns the abstract statement 'that he had an equivalent centre of self' into an experience that has 'the directness of sense'—'whence the lights and shadows must always fall with a certain difference'.

The same distinction—between 'the commonplace' and 'the acute consciousness'—is at the centre of this paragraph, which describes Casaubon's response to Lydgate's warning that he may die suddenly at any moment:

Lydgate, certain that his patient wished to be alone, soon left him; and the black figure with hands behind and head bent forward continued to pace the walk where the dark yew trees gave him a mute companionship in melancholy, and the little shadows of bird or leaf that fleeted across the isles of sunlight, stole along in silence as in the presence of a sorrow. Here was a man who now for the first time found himself looking into the eyes of death—who was passing through one of those rare moments of experience when we feel the truth of a commonplace, which is as different from what we call knowing it, as the vision of waters upon the earth is different from the delirious vision of the water which cannot be had to cool the burning tongue. When the commonplace 'We must all die' transforms itself suddenly into the acute consciousness 'I must die—and soon', then death grapples us, and his fingers are cruel; afterwards, he may come to fold us in his arms as our mother did, and our last moment of dim earthly discerning may be like the first. To Mr. Casaubon now, it was as if he suddenly found himself on the dark river-brink and heard the plash of the oncoming oar, not discerning the forms, but expecting the summons. In such an hour the mind does not change its lifelong bias, but carries it onward in imagination to the other side of death, gazing backward—perhaps with the divine calm of beneficence, perhaps with the petty anxieties of self-assertion. What was Mr. Casaubon's bias his acts will give us a clue to. He held himself to be, with some private scholarly reservations, a believing Christian, as to estimates of the present and hopes of the future. But what we strive to gratify, though we may call it a distant hope, is an immediate desire; the future estate for which men drudge up city alleys exists already in their imagination and love. And Mr. Casaubon's immediate desire was not for divine communion and light divested of earthly conditions; his passionate longings, poor man, clung low and mist-like in very shady places. (I, 375)

The paragraph is at the same time a demonstration of the operation of the sympathetic imagination, entering to the 'centre of self' of another person. At first we watch Casaubon from a distance as he walks away from us; his surroundings suggest the background that must colour his thoughts. We know what he has just been told; the next two sentences dwell on the effect such knowledge might be expected to have on ourselves, and turn the abstract statement into the tangible realities of 'death grapples us' and 'fold us in his arms as our mother did'. From this consideration of what such knowledge might mean to any of us, we move on to the form it might be expected to take for Mr Casaubon: the mythological form of the Styx, river of death, and the oars of Charon the ferryman. Perhaps for the first time in his experience, a part of the mythology that he knows so much about has come to have real meaning for him. The paragraph closes with a contrast between his formal and intellectual belief and his 'passionate longings', and by this time we do not suspect any irony or condescension in the expression 'poor man'.

The treatment of Will Ladislaw in the novel seems to me to be unsatisfactory, and to fail to achieve that attachment and detachment that give the other important characters in the novel their three-dimensional quality. For this reason I shall say very little about him and the parts of the novel in which he plays an important part, because although his role is conceived as significantly related to Dorothea's, his presence is in fact ineffectual.

The first impression on seeing Will was one of sunny brightness, which added to the uncertainty of his changing expression. Surely, his very features changed their form; his jaw looked sometimes large and sometimes small;

and the little ripple in his nose was a preparation for metamorphosis. When he turned his head quickly his hair seemed to shake out light, and some persons thought they saw decided genius in this coruscation. Mr. Casaubon, on the contrary, stood rayless. (I, 184)

There is an uncertainty in the description, and George Eliot fails to pass it off as a precise description of a quality of uncertainty in the man. The passage offers us, not an account of Ladislaw, but a way of seeing him: the way of a woman who is in love with him. Despite the gesture towards objective detachment in 'some persons thought they saw', the description is of the person one adores, a person to whom one can hardly bear to attribute any specific virtue or beauty in case it should exclude a conflicting one. What is embarrassing is that George Eliot does not seem to realize this; she does not give us this description as Dorothea's impression, but as if it were what any observer would notice— as if Casaubon himself would see him in this way. And in the following passage of conversation, she evidently expects the reader to share her delight:

'You *are* a poem—and that is to be the best part of a poet—what makes up the poet's consciousness in his best moods', said Will, showing such originality as we all share with the morning and the spring-time and other endless renewals.

'I am very glad to hear it', said Dorothea, laughing out her words in a birdlike modulation, and looking at Will with playful gratitude in her eyes. 'What very kind things you say to me!'

'I wish I could ever do anything that would be what you call kind—that I could ever be of the slightest service to you. I fear I shall never have the opportunity.' Will spoke with fervour. (I, 198)

This variant of 'courtly love' is in a Romantic fashion (not yet dead, perhaps) most concisely exemplified in Shelley's poem:

One word is too often profaned
 For me to profane it,
One feeling too falsely disdained
 For thee to disdain it;
One hope is too like despair
 For prudence to smother,
And pity from thee more dear
 Than that from another.

I can give not what men call love,
 But wilt thou accept not

The worship the heart lifts above
And the Heavens reject not,—
The desire of the moth for the star,
Of the night for the morrow,
The devotion to something afar
From the sphere of our sorrow?

Here, if anywhere, we need the effective presence of some such voice as Mrs Cadwallader's, or perhaps Mr Brooke's 'That kind of thing is not healthy, my dear.'

By the standards that this novel establishes, Ladislaw hardly exists; but he serves a purpose—his voice, which might be almost anybody's voice, the voice of malice with ulterior motives, is such a voice as Dorothea must, sometime or other, encounter. Her love for Casaubon, founded on admiration—which is a form of judgment—is vulnerable (as sympathy is not) to the kind of evidence and argument that can modify judgment; and Casaubon has given it no opportunity to turn into a more secure feeling, reinforced by shared physical tenderness. And her new intimate knowledge of him predisposes her to be attentive to the evidence, however unreliable, of his detractors.

If we say that George Eliot is not in full command of her art— that her intelligence is not fully effective—in her treatment of Will Ladislaw, we must remember that we are judging by the highest standards: those established by this novel. The scene in which Mary Garth is in attendance on old Featherstone during the last hours of his life is one in which standards are created; it is great art, and wholly characteristic of George Eliot. Its strength is in the intelligence of the author; it is not a matter of using techniques to produce certain effects on the reader.

She sat to-night revolving, as she was wont, the scenes of the day, her lips often curling with amusement at the oddities to which her fancy added fresh drollery: people were so ridiculous with their illusions, carrying their fool's caps unawares, thinking their own lies opaque while everybody else's were transparent, making themselves exceptions to everything, as if when all the world looked yellow under a lamp they alone were rosy. Yet there were some illusions under Mary's eyes which were not quite comic to her. She was secretly convinced, though she had no other grounds than her close observation of old Featherstone's nature, that in spite of his fondness for having the

Vincys about him, they were as likely to be disappointed as any of the relations whom he kept at a distance. She had a good deal of disdain for Mrs. Vincy's evident alarm lest she and Fred should be alone together, but it did not hinder her from thinking anxiously of the way in which Fred would be affected, if it should turn out that his uncle had left him as poor as ever. She could make a butt of Fred when he was present, but she did not enjoy his follies when he was absent.

Yet she liked her thoughts: a vigorous young mind not over-balanced by passion, finds a good in making acquaintance with life, and watches its own powers with interest. Mary had plenty of merriment within.

Her thought was not veined by any solemnity or pathos about the old man on the bed: such sentiments are easier to affect than to feel about an aged creature whose life is not visibly anything but a remnant of vices. She had always seen the most disagreeable side of Mr. Featherstone: he was not proud of her, and she was only useful to him. To be anxious about a soul that is always snapping at you must be left to the saints of the earth; and Mary was not one of them. She had never returned him a harsh word, and had waited on him faithfully: that was her utmost. Old Featherstone himself was not in the least anxious about his soul, and had declined to see Mr. Tucker on the subject.   (I, 278)

Like all great art, it has a liberating effect. There are certain feelings that we are accustomed to believe we ought to feel on certain occasions, notably when somebody is dying. We are consequently embarrassed when we find that we do not in fact feel them, and that our minds are wandering in a way that seems frivolous. The final absurdity, of course, is that each person tends to suspect that only he is responding so inappropriately; it is a kind of embarrassment that isolates people from each other. This is one way in which art breaks down barriers between people: it can help them to recognize and accept their own secret feelings as perfectly natural—as feelings that the artist too has experienced, and been able to express. D. H. Lawrence says that a critic 'must have the courage to admit what he feels, as well as the flexibility to *know* what he feels', and this applies to the creative artist as well. Mary's lack of 'solemnity and pathos about the old man on the bed' is shown as natural, and offered for our approval; it is evidence of 'a vigorous young mind'.

Far from being used to move the reader to tears, or to inspire awe, the death of Featherstone is made (characteristically) the occasion for a moral problem. This is later summarized, by

Caleb Garth; and his comments explore a further dimension of morality:

'Now, you see, the will he wanted burnt was this last, so that if Mary had done what he wanted, Fred Vincy would have had ten thousand pounds. The old man did turn to him at the last. That touches poor Mary close; she couldn't help it—she was in the right to do what she did, but she feels, as she says, much as if she had knocked down somebody's property and broken it against her will, when she was rightfully defending herself. I feel with her, somehow, and if I could make any amends to the poor lad, instead of bearing him a grudge for the harm he did us, I should be glad to do it. Now, what is your opinion, sir? Susan doesn't agree with me, She says—tell what you say, Susan.'

'Mary could not have acted otherwise, even if she had known what would be the effect on Fred', said Mrs. Garth, pausing from her work, and looking at Mr. Farebrother. 'And she was quite ignorant of it. It seems to me, a loss which falls on another because we have done right is not to lie upon our conscience.'

The Vicar did not answer immediately, and Caleb said, 'It's the feeling. The child feels in that way, and I feel with her. You don't mean your horse to tread on a dog when you're backing out of the way; but it goes through you, when it's done.' (I, 359)

If one incurs guilt through one's own fault, one can repent and seek forgiveness; but it is more difficult to deal with guilt innocently incurred. The Greek tragedians knew about such guilt; but later moralists have been inclined to ignore it, stressing the quality of the intention, rather than the actual consequences of the action. George Eliot has said earlier, about Fred Vincy,

Indeed we are most of us brought up in the notion that the highest motive for not doing a wrong is something irrespective of the beings who would suffer the wrong. (I, 218)

She recognizes that it is from the actual consequences of our actions that we incur guilt; although the impossibility of doing otherwise can justify the actions, it cannot do away with the sense of guilt.

This is one of the dimensions that make it inappropriate to talk of 'moral problems' in *Middlemarch*, if by 'problem' we imply that there is a solution, accessible to intelligence and good-will. It would be more precise to call them 'moral predicaments', and they have no right answer—there are only decisions to be made, on uncertain grounds. The decisions may be better or worse, and they may turn out well or badly, but they are rarely simply right or wrong.

It is characteristic of the structure of this novel that Mary Garth's refusal to do what the dying Featherstone demands is balanced by Dorothea's decision to do what the dying Casaubon asks. The circumstances are very different, and we might almost suppose that the presence of both scenes in the same book was— if not mere chance—only a structural elegance. But they seem to me to be a pair of matched observations that, together, convey a warning against generalizing inappropriately. There is, for example, a good deal of 'solemnity and pathos' in Dorothea's feeling about Casaubon, and they are not at all inappropriate— though similar feelings would have been inappropriate and merely conventional in Mary Garth. In Dorothea the pathos becomes sympathy, and we are shown how much nearer Dorothea has come to feeling with Casaubon:

> And here Dorothea's pity turned from her own future to her husband's past—nay, to his present hard struggle with a lot which had grown out of the past: the lonely labour, the ambition breathing hardly under the pressure of self-distrust; the goal receding, and the heavier limbs; and now at last the sword visibly trembling above him! And had she not wished to marry him that she might help him in his life's labour?—But she had thought the work was to be something greater, which she could serve in devoutly for its own sake. Was it right, even to soothe his grief—would it be possible, even if she promised—to work as in a treadmill fruitlessly?...
>
> And now, if she were to say, 'No! if you die, I will put no finger to your work'—it seemed as if she would be crushing that bruised heart. (II, 45)

There is no right answer, no solution to the problem; the clearer it becomes, the more impossible it is seen to be.

> For four hours Dorothea lay in this conflict, till she felt ill and bewildered, unable to resolve, praying mutely. (II, 46)

The decision she has reached in the morning is an expression of her own character, rather than the logical outcome of her reflections on the problem: it is a choice, not a solution. A final, almost intolerable complexity is given to the episode by Casaubon's dying before she can give him the promise she has resolved to give; is she still bound by it?

But in spite of the final twist, and the fact that Dorothea does not know what Casaubon had intended to require of her, the reasonable analysis of her predicament is valuable. The description of Dorothea's conflicting thoughts and feelings—which is cool and precise without distorting the thoughts and feelings by suggesting that *they* are cool and precise—is a demonstration of the part that reason can have in a moral choice, although it cannot give one right answer.

I have suggested that we see in the novel a growth in Dorothea's sympathy, her power to feel with Casaubon even while she sees his failure clearly. There are several scenes that illustrate a corresponding broadening of her sympathy with other people, more ordinary than herself; so that as the novel progresses it traces in Dorothea a growth into the fullness of the humanity that she shares with others, without any loss of unique individuality. In the beginning of Book VI there is still a need for the kind of criticism that Mrs Cadwallader is best fitted to make—we recognize the element of truth in it, and delight in it, though it is clearly not an authoritative judgment.

Mrs. Cadwallader said, privately, 'You will certainly go mad in that house alone, my dear. You will see visions. We have all got to exert ourselves a little to keep sane, and call things by the same names as other people call them by. To be sure, for younger sons and women who have no money, it is a sort of provision to go mad: they are taken care of then. But you must not run into that. I daresay you are a little bored here with our good dowager; but think what a bore you might become yourself to your fellow-creatures if you were always playing tragedy queen and taking things sublimely. Sitting alone in that library at Lowick you may fancy yourself ruling the weather; you must get a few people round you who wouldn't believe you if you told them. That is a good lowering medicine.' (II, 95)

In fact Mrs Cadwallader does not have the last word in this exchange, and Dorothea reserves her right as a thinking individual to 'think that the greater part of the world is mistaken about many things'. Again it is the continual awareness of different ways of judging—none infallible, but none entirely negligible—that distinguishes George Eliot; it is her sense of opposing yet complementary truths that underlies the texture of her prose and the structure of the novel.

A very important part of the structure, of course, is the grouping of several marriages so that each throws light on the others. I have already referred to Rosamond's and Dorothea's choices—a suggestion of ominous similarities between their two modes, apparently so different, of 'falling in love'. Without undertaking a comprehensive account of the relationship between Lydgate and Rosamond, I want to point to some aspects of it.

Lydgate's tragedy is the failure of his admirable hopes—largely as a result of his marriage with Rosamond. But there is some justice in her reply here, at the end of the novel:

He once called her his basil plant; and when she asked for an explanation, said that basil was a plant which had flourished wonderfully on a murdered man's brains. Rosamond had a placid but strong answer to such speeches. Why then had he chosen her? (II, 361)

Of course her reply has, in the first place, a *dramatic* rightness: when Lydgate talks like that he has to be answered sharply. But it has a further justice: there *is* no escape from responsibility, however blindly incurred, by blaming somebody else.

Lydgate's weakness, and the inevitability that he will compromise with 'the world' (social and financial pressures) has been indicated before Rosamond can possibly be held responsible—in his voting for Tyke against Farebrother. There he yielded to social pressures in the very act of making a gesture of defiance of them, a gesture that gives him the excuse he *wants* for voting against his conscience; but his weakness is most clearly evident before the meeting, when he chooses not to decide which way he will vote—

without telling himself the reason, he deferred the predetermination on which side he should give his vote. (I, 155)

There are relevant comparisons to be made with other decisions made in the novel; Dorothea's, for example, to give Casaubon the promise he asks for. What Lydgate does is deliberately defer a decision—

his hope was really in the chance that discussion might somehow give a new aspect to the question, and make the scale dip so as to exclude the necessity for voting. I think he trusted a little also to the energy which is begotten by circumstances—some feeling rushing warmly and making resolve easy, while debate in cool blood had only made it more difficult. (I, 158)

The habit of mind that postpones a difficult decision in the hope that the need for it may go away, or that circumstances may make it easy, is very different from that which leads Dorothea to consider every aspect of the choice with which she is confronted. In both cases the decision may finally be an impulsive one, but Dorothea's impulse is her response to the whole considered dilemma whereas Lydgate's is an evasion of consideration. For Dorothea, circumstances *do* finally make her sacrifice unnecessary —but the fact that events do often (as George Eliot shows) take our decisions out of our hands does not justify a habit of trusting that they will. In fact, of course, Lydgate cannot evade the responsibility for his choice by leaving it to circumstances to make it for him; in choosing not to choose, he has made a moral choice and is responsible for its consequences.

Lydgate at least *has* a choice in the matter, and bears the responsibility for it; Rosamond strikes us as hardly having any choice or responsibility. It is Celia, not Rosamond, who is described as being,

if it were not doctrinally wrong to say so, hardly more in need of salvation than a squirrel. (I, 26)

but Rosamond too is described in terms of plants and animals—

her flower-like head on its white stem. (I, 101)

But she...turned her long neck a little, and put up her hand to touch her wondrous hair-plaits—an habitual gesture with her as pretty as any movements of a kitten's paw. (I, 139)

'Yes, certainly I hear you', said Rosamond, turning her head aside with the movement of a graceful long-necked bird. (II, 291)

he gained a good income, and instead of the threatened cage in Bride Street provided one all flowers and gilding, fit for the bird of paradise that she resembled. (II, 360)

(I am tempted to add Dr F. R. Leavis's remark in *The Great Tradition* which is so aptly responsive that it has almost become for me a part of the novel:

the reader...catches himself, from time to time, wanting to break that graceful neck, the turns of which, as George Eliot evokes them, convey both infuriating obstinacy and a sinister hint of the snake.)

The image of the squirrel applied to Celia has a very different effect: it suggests her 'natural' wholeness, her fortunate exemption

89

from destructive opposition between the life of the spirit and her biological destiny as a woman. Rosamond's beauty is defined by the imagery of flower, animal and bird as less than fully human, inaccessible to reason—yet retaining in full the human capacity for destruction. If Lydgate compromises with the world, Rosamond has nothing to compromise. Not that she is mercenary; that would be unladylike:

There was nothing financial, still less sordid, in her previsions: she cared about what were considered refinements, and not about the money that was to pay for them. (I, 103)

—she only wants, or rather she takes for granted, things that cost money. The money itself was only 'something necessary which other people would always provide'. Given the limitations of her intellect and her almost total lack of sympathetic imagination, it is hard to blame her, though one shudders. 'What can *I* do, Tertius?' she asks; and the words, with their inflexion of 'the most neutral aloofness', summarize her placid helplessness.

One can hardly read George Eliot's novels without confronting, on several occasions, the question of determinism. When a writer presents so fully the quality of a mind and the forces, external and internal, that impel it to a decision, it is hard to avoid the suspicion that no other decision would have been possible. The general philosophic question need not stop us now; we are not likely to find an answer to it. Perhaps it will be enough for our present purpose—for reading the novels—to observe that there, as in the life around us, some people appear to be far more 'free' than others. If we take the convenient terms of the verse—

> There was a young man who said, 'Damn!
> I am perfectly sure that I am
> A creature that moves
> In predestined grooves,
> In fact, not a bus, but a tram!'

—we might say that, in *Middlemarch*, Rosamond is pre-eminently a tram. She is little more than a social mechanism, and her response to any situation becomes predictable. Can a tram become free?—Only, the novel suggests, if derailed by a bus.

Perhaps if he had been strong enough to persist in his determination to be the more because she was less, that evening might have had a better issue. If his energy could have borne down that check, he might still have wrought on Rosamond's vision and will. We cannot be sure that any natures, however inflexible or peculiar, will resist this effect from a more massive being than their own. They may be taken by storm and for the moment converted, becoming part of the soul which enwraps them in the ardour of its movement. But poor Lydgate had a throbbing pain within him, and his energy had fallen short of its task.   (II, 295)

Lydgate does not derail Rosamond; Dorothea, however briefly, does, after Ladislaw's anger has begun the process—

It was a newer crisis in Rosamond's experience than even Dorothea could imagine: she was under the first great shock that had shattered her dream-world in which she had been easily confident of herself and critical of others; and this strange unexpected manifestation of feeling in a woman whom she had approached with a shrinking aversion and dread, as one who must necessarily have a jealous hatred towards her, made her soul totter all the more with a sense that she had been walking in an unknown world which had just broken in upon her.   (II, 328)

But a derailed tram does not become a bus; Rosamond does not turn into a brave free spirit.

'How heavy your eyes are, Tertius—and do push your hair back.' He lifted up his large white hand to obey her, and felt thankful for this little mark of interest in him. Poor Rosamond's vagrant fancy had come back terribly scourged—meek enough to nestle under the old despised shelter. And the shelter was still there: Lydgate had accepted his narrowed lot with sad resignation. He had chosen this fragile creature, and had taken the burthen of her life upon his arms. He must walk as he could, carrying that burthen pitifully.   (II, 331)

Nor, indeed, is Lydgate a free spirit—although he is sufficiently free to be responsible for his actions, as Rosamond hardly is for hers. His choice of Rosamond is not only a response to her flower-like beauty. It is at the same time a recognition of certain fundamental affinities between them. We have already seen, when Lydgate yields to immediate pressures in voting for Tyke, how he reveals a susceptibility to such pressures and even deliberately exposes himself to them. His habitual extravagance is not very different from Rosamond's:

Rosamond, accustomed from her childhood to an extravagant household, thought that good housekeeping consisted simply in ordering the best of everything—nothing else 'answered'; and Lydgate supposed that 'if things were done at all, they must be done properly'—he did not see how they were to live otherwise...Lydgate believed himself to be careless about his dress, and he despised a man who calculated the effects of his costume; it seemed to him only a matter of course that he had abundance of fresh garments—such things were naturally ordered in sheaves. (II, 141)

With Rosamond's failure to appreciate Lydgate's dedication to his professional ideals, we must confront his unreasonable expectation that she should: he bears patiently

the blank unreflecting surface her mind presented to his ardour for the more impersonal ends of his profession and his scientific study, an ardour which he had fancied that the ideal wife must somehow worship as sublime, though not in the least knowing why. (II, 140)

We can hardly fail to recall, as an ironical commentary, Casaubon's expectation of uncritical devotion—just as, while we applaud Lydgate's assertion that Rosamond must learn to take his judgment on questions she doesn't understand, our approval is moderated by the recollection of Casaubon's

'Dorothea, my love, this is not the first occasion, but it were well that it should be the last, on which you have assumed a judgment on subjects beyond your scope...' (I, 330)

—to which our response has been quite different.

The failure of a relationship—particularly of such a close relationship as marriage—is, the novel suggests, the failure of both persons. The failure of one person to understand is inseparable from the other's failure to communicate.

Lydgate, then, has weaknesses— 'spots of commonness'— that are closely related to those of the woman he has chosen to marry. What is admirable in him is obvious enough; what I want to call attention to now is the weakness that links him with Rosamond. He is trapped by circumstances in ways with which we can easily sympathize—

What could he do? He could not see a man sink close to him for want of help. He rose and gave his arm to Bulstrode... (III, 270)

—but that 'What could he do?' is related to Rosamond's 'What can *I* do, Tertius?' However vividly George Eliot presents the compelling power of circumstances, we remain aware that

It always remains true that if we had been greater, circumstances would have been less strong against us. (II, 140)

Rather as the relationship between Casaubon and Dorothea illuminates, and is illuminated by, that between Lydgate and Rosamond, the moral problem of Bulstrode throws light on Lydgate's. But here the illumination comes in a different way. The two marriages lead our sympathies in different directions in situations that have, theoretically, much in common. They thus make us duly hesitant to generalize, as either alone might prompt us to do, on the proper relationship between a man, his marriage and his work. But Bulstrode's compromises with evil in the hope that good may come of it are more directly connected with Lydgate's compromises. Bulstrode's are an exaggeration of Lydgate's and illuminate them in that way. Besides, the thing that Lydgate compromises with *is* Bulstrode. His association with Bulstrode is a shameful one; although he has no certain knowledge of the dishonourable source of Bulstrode's fortune until late in the novel, he feels—but refuses to admit to himself—that there is something dishonourable in the way he allows himself to become gradually dependent on him.

Like Lydgate, Bulstrode can tell himself at every stage that he could not have done otherwise.

But the train of causes in which he had locked himself went on. (II, 168)

This suggests a modified determinism. Even while George Eliot recognizes the necessary sequence of cause and effect, she denies us the excuse that we have had no choice. The implication of the sentence I have quoted is that the chain of causes *does* exist, but that each of us is personally responsible for allowing ourselves to be chained. This may be philosophically inconsistent, but it is true to experience, and it is applicable to Lydgate as well as to Bulstrode.

Bulstrode's sense of inevitability, however, expresses itself in his consciousness in different terms from Lydgate's. Lydgate is a scientist, and his sense of inevitability is that of a scientist; Bulstrode's clothes itself in the language of the evangelical

Christian, and sees himself sometimes as being led by Providence, and sometimes—here, for example—as excluded from grace and being used 'instrumentally' by Providence in its care for others:

There were hours in which Bulstrode felt that his action was unrighteous; but how could he go back? He had mental exercises, called himself nought, and went on in his course of instrumentality...

The spiritual kind of rescue was a genuine need with him. There may be coarse hypocrites, who consciously affect beliefs and emotions for the sake of gulling the world, but Bulstrode was not one of them.   (II, 169, 170)

The achievement of sympathy with, and understanding of, such a man as Bulstrode is one of the most impressive in fiction; it is not properly represented by the fragments I have quoted, because in the novel it comes as a sharp reversal of our sympathies when we have become accustomed to seeing Bulstrode as an evil influence in Lydgate's life rather than as a suffering man in his own right. And what makes the understanding especially impressive is that it does not negate our judgment of Bulstrode; it demonstrates how moral judgment can be at the same time rigorous and charitable.

Marriage is, of course, a central concern of this novel; and one of the most moving of its presentations of moments that illuminate the quality of the various relationships comes when Bulstrode awaits his wife's reaction to the gossip about him.

It was eight o'clock in the evening before the door opened and his wife entered. He dared not look up at her. He sat with his eyes bent down, and as she went towards him she thought he looked smaller—he seemed so withered and shrunken. A movement of new compassion and old tenderness went through her like a great wave, and putting one hand on his which rested on the arm of the chair, and the other on his shoulder, she said, solemnly but kindly—

'Look up, Nicholas.'

He raised his eyes with a little start and looked at her half amazed for a moment: her pale face, her changed, mourning dress, the trembling about her mouth, all said, 'I know'; and her hands and eyes rested gently on him. He burst out crying and they cried together, she sitting at his side. They could not yet speak to each other of the shame which she was bearing with him, or of the acts which had brought it down on them. His confession was silent, and her promise of faithfulness was silent. Open-minded as she was, she nevertheless shrank from the words which would have expressed their mutual consciousness as she would have shrunk from flakes of fire. She could not say, 'How much is only slander, and false suspicion?' and he did not say, 'I am innocent.'   (II, 288)

Very soon after this we see Lydgate waiting for Rosamond's reaction.

The next two days Lydgate observed a change in her, and believed that she had heard the bad news. Would she speak to him about it, or would she go on for ever in the silence which seemed to imply that she believed him guilty? We must remember that he was in a morbid state of mind, in which almost all contact was pain. Certainly Rosamond in this case had equal reason to complain of reserve and want of confidence on his part; but in the bitterness of his soul he excused himself;—was he not justified in shrinking from the task of telling her, since now she knew the truth she had no impulse to speak to him? But a deeper-lying consciousness that he was in fault made him restless, and the silence between them became intolerable to him; it was as if they were both adrift on one piece of wreck and looked away from each other.

He thought, 'I am a fool. Haven't I given up expecting anything? I have married care, not help.' And that evening he said—

'Rosamond, have you heard anything that distresses you?'

'Yes', she answered, laying down her work, which she had been carrying on with a languid semi-consciousness, most unlike her usual self.

'What have you heard?'

'Everything, I suppose. Papa told me.'

'That people think me disgraced?'

'Yes', said Rosamond, faintly, beginning to sew again automatically.

There was silence. Lydgate thought, 'If she has any trust in me—any notion of what I am, she ought to speak now and say that she does not believe I have deserved disgrace.'

But Rosamond on her side went on moving her fingers languidly. Whatever was to be said on the subject she expected to come from Tertius. What did she know? And if he were innocent of any wrong, why did he not do something to clear himself? (II, 293)

Both scenes end in silences; the difference between them focusses the difference between Bulstrode's and Lydgate's marriages. Even when the reader has been drawn so far towards sympathetic understanding of Bulstrode, it comes as something of a shock that he, of all the husbands in the novel, should be blessed with the silence that is more communicative than speech. Obviously George Eliot is not interested in rewarding the good, the wise and the beautiful. But there may be some relation between this triumph of Bulstrode's marriage and the fullness of the suffering through which he has passed.

A great deal of *Middlemarch* remains to be discussed. Mary

Garth is impressive, but not sufficiently present in the novel to stand as a representative of a kind of femininity comparable with Dorothea's. Celia disappears from the novel, although she too has important qualities that seem at first to be fruitful sources of implicit and explicit comparisons with Dorothea. It is not hard for Dorothea to rise superior to her sex, if that is represented mainly by Rosamond. But when we have experienced such a variety of comparative valuations, when our sympathies have been led in so many unaccustomed directions, it would be absurd to end this account of the novel with a regret that it has not achieved even more.

At the beginning of this commentary on the novel, I used a stanza from Gray's *Elegy Written in a Country Churchyard* to focus the mode of feeling that seems implicit in the 'Prelude' to the novel, a mode that some critics see as predominant in the novel as a whole, with special reference to Dorothea:

> Full many a gem of purest ray serene
>   The dark unfathom'd caves of ocean bear;
> Full many a flower is born to blush unseen
>   And waste its sweetness on the desert air.

George Eliot at her best deals with *that* point of view here:

The auctioneer burst out in deep remonstrance—
'Ah! Mr. Ladislaw! the frame alone is worth that. Ladies and gentlemen, for the credit of the town! Suppose it should be discovered hereafter that a gem of art has been amongst us in this town, and nobody in Middlemarch awake to it. Five guineas—five seven-six—five ten. Still, ladies, still! It is a gem, and 'Full many a gem', as the poet says, has been allowed to go at a nominal price because the public knew no better, because it was offered in circles where there was—I was going to say a low feeling, but no!—Six pounds—six guineas—a *Guydo* of the first order going at six guineas—it is an insult to religion, ladies; it touches us all as Christians, gentlemen, that a subject like this should go at such a low figure—six pounds ten—seven—'

(II, 160)

This is evidently an ironical comment on the *Elegy*; less certainly, but arguably, it is a comment on the kind of feeling that the 'Prelude' encourages. And one would like to believe that George Eliot recognized its comment on the related fact that it is Ladislaw who brings the proper market price for the gem, the religious painting of the first order, that is Dorothea.

7

DANIEL DERONDA[1]

Most of George Eliot's novels begin by creating the place in which the action is to pass. For the reader, if not always for the central character, there is from the start a piece of ground where, for the duration of the novel, he has his roots. The place and the time establish the conditions for the action, the range of possibilities within which moral choices are to be made and judged. This novel, on the other hand, opens with a chance encounter in a place remote from the scenes of the action that follows; the establishment of a scene for a substantial part of the novel comes only in the third chapter, and concerns itself with rootedness only to deplore Gwendolen's lack of it.

> Pity that Offendene was not the home of Miss Harleth's childhood, or endeared to her by family memories! A human life, I think, should be well rooted in some spot of a native land, where it may get the love of tender kinship for the face of earth, for the labours men go forth to, for the sounds and accents that haunt it, for whatever will give that early home a familiar unmistakable difference amidst the future widening of knowledge: a spot where the definiteness of early memories may be inwrought with affection, and kindly acquaintance with all neighbours, even to the dogs and donkeys, may spread not by sentimental effort and reflection, but as a sweet habit of the blood...
>
> But this blessed persistence in which affection can take root had been wanting in Gwendolen's life. (12)

Neither this theme, nor this tone, has much further part in *Daniel Deronda*. In this, her last novel, George Eliot's concern is with kinds of rootedness that are not, for the individual, a matter of 'some spot of a native land'. Certainly, for Deronda and Mirah,

---

[1] I have as usual given page-references to the Everyman edition, which is in two volumes but numbers its pages consecutively (1–300 are in vol. I, 301–612 in vol. II). In this case, however, the page-numbers are the same as those of the Harper Torchbooks edition, which has a valuable introduction by F. R. Leavis; it is a paperback, and is thus cheaper than the Everyman, but will not stand repeated readings.

the destinies they choose for themselves as individuals lead them to a place that they regard as the homeland of their race, but it is not a place that they have been familiar with in childhood.

It will be useful to recall, in considering the treatment of Gwendolen Harleth, a formulation from *Middlemarch*: 'We are all of us born in moral stupidity, taking the world as an udder to feed our supreme selves.' Gwendolen, whose childhood has not included the educative familiarity with one 'dear perpetual place', has also been nurtured in this moral stupidity by an over-indulgent mother, who seems positively to encourage her to see everyone and everything in terms of her own convenience.

It was always arranged, when possible, that she should have a small bed in her mamma's room; for Mrs. Davilow's motherly tenderness clung chiefly to her eldest girl, who had been born in her happier time. One night under an attack of pain she found that the specific regularly placed by her bedside had been forgotten, and begged Gwendolen to get out of bed and reach it for her. That healthy young lady, snug and warm as a rosy infant in her little couch, objected to step out into the cold, and lying perfectly still, grumbled a refusal. Mrs. Davilow went without the medicine and never reproached her daughter; but the next day Gwendolen was keenly conscious of what must be in her mamma's mind, and tried to make amends by caresses which cost her no effort.
(14)

The incident makes it as clear as anything could what 'moral stupidity' means, and we are in no danger of excusing it in Gwendolen when George Eliot goes on to account for it as a consequence of the way she is treated:

Having always been the pet and pride of the household, waited on by mother, sisters, governess, and maids, as if she had been a princess in exile, she naturally found it difficult to think her own pleasure less important than others made it.
(14)

In fact we are not allowed to rest in such an account, which would tend to shift the responsibility for Gwendolen's defect to her mother and sisters; we are led to question further, and to see that their treatment of her must, in its turn, be accounted for, and is to be attributed to something in her. It may be partly

her beauty, a certain unusualness about her, a decision of will which made itself felt in her graceful movements and clear unhesitating tones (27)

but it is also a certain ruthlessness,

a strong determination to have what was pleasant, with a total fearlessness in making [herself] disagreeable or dangerous when [she] did not get it.

(28)

The deliberate circularity of this chain of cause and effect helps to establish very early in the novel that to know all is not to forgive all. As for Gwendolen herself, the introductory account leaves us with 'the iridescence of her character—the play of various, nay, contrary tendencies'. The attempt to account for her character seems to be there largely in order to show that such theorizing is unlikely to throw much fresh light on her, and, despite its precision and logical coherence, is left behind as if in haste to proceed with the narration of events. For it is in the narration, the creation of significant incident and the language in which it is presented, that this novel conveys its most acute moral perceptions.

It is direct narrative, rather than explicit commentary, that gives us the precise quality of Gwendolen's 'iridescence'—the quick fancy, the capacity for delight that almost repays those who are sacrificed, and sacrifice themselves, to sustain it. The family has just entered the house that is to be their new home.

'Mamma, mamma, pray come here!' said Gwendolen, Mrs. Davilow having followed slowly in talk with the housekeeper. 'Here is an organ: I will be Saint Cecilia: some one shall paint me as Saint Cecilia. Jocosa (this was her name for Miss Merry), let down my hair. See, mamma!'

She had thrown off her hat and gloves, and seated herself before the organ in an admirable pose, looking upward; while the submissive and sad Jocosa took out the one comb which fastened the coil of hair, and then shook out the mass till it fell in a smooth light-brown stream far below its owner's slim waist.

Mrs. Davilow smiled and said, 'A charming picture, my dear!' not indifferent to the display of her pet, even in the presence of a housekeeper. Gwendolen rose and laughed with delight. All this seemed quite to the purpose on entering a new house which was so excellent a background.

(16)

That other activities might be rather more to the purpose on entering a new house is made plain enough, without comment, by the barely presented fact of Mrs Davilow in talk with the housekeeper, so that Gwendolen's merely aesthetic appreciation of the house—as an 'excellent...background' (for her performances) is ironically placed. The irony, though, being thus implicitly pointed, is delicately limited in its effect, so that we still recognize Gwendolen's pose as 'admirable'—a product, however trivial, of some kind of intelligence that her mother and sisters lack.

Immediately after this there is a surprising indication of possible emotional depth in Gwendolen—again in a significant incident presented with a minimum of comment.

'Oh *Gwendolen*!' said the small Isabel, in a tone of astonishment, while she held open a hinged panel of the wainscot at the other end of the room.

Everyone, Gwendolen first, went to look. The opened panel had disclosed the picture of an upturned dead face, from which an obscure figure seemed to be fleeing with outstretched arms. 'How horrible!' said Mrs. Davilow, with a look of mere disgust; but Gwendolen shuddered silently, and Isabel, a plain and altogether inconvenient child with an alarming memory, said—

'You will never stay in this room by yourself, Gwendolen.'   (16)

Gwendolen's silent shudder, contrasting with Isabel's 'tone of astonishment' and Mrs Davilow's 'look of mere disgust', is the guarantee that, for all her cool poise, she is capable of a certain depth of emotional response. For her it is inconvenient—it spoils her performance (as the same picture does again later), and she can only express her feelings in the form of extreme irritation. On both occasions the incidents have their significance as diagnosis, and as warnings that Gwendolen cannot take—warnings of the error in her calculations when she decides to marry Grandcourt: what is to make her unable to dominate him as she plans to do is her unacknowledged capacity for real feeling. Without it she would be invulnerable, as Grandcourt himself is, and could be a match for him: but in her marriage, as in these incidents, her feelings will spoil her performance.

Gwendolen's tendency to underestimate the understanding of other people, another aspect of the limitation of her intelligence, is dramatized in her conversation with Mrs Arrowpoint—her hostess on this occasion—who writes books. 'I understand you are an accomplished singer', Mrs Arrowpoint has just said.

'Oh no!—"die Kraft ist schwach, allein die Lust ist gross"', as Mephistopheles says.'

'Ah, you are a student of Goethe. Young ladies are so advanced now. I suppose you have read everything.'

'No, really. I shall be so glad if you will tell me what to read. I have been looking into all the books in the library at Offendene, but there is nothing readable. The leaves all stick together and smell musty. I wish I could write books to amuse myself, as you can! How delightful it must be to write books after one's own taste instead of reading other people's! Home-made books must be so nice.' (30)

What follows shows that Gwendolen has gone only a shade too far, so as to arouse a momentary suspicion of her ironical intention in Mrs Arrowpoint; her tone has been such as to enable her to revert instantly to the 'girlish simplicity' of 'I would give any-thing to write a book!' But her weakness is revealed to the reader: an excessive delight in her own cleverness that leads her to underrate the intelligence of others, and to behave as if she were performing before an admiring audience even when there is none but herself. It is even, one feels at this point, a kind of vulgarity, so that one is led to use the limiting word 'cleverness' rather than 'intelligence'.

But again our view of her is modified when we find her capable of feeling humiliation, after the music-teacher Herr Klesmer has commented on her singing, 'at the sudden width of horizon opened round her small musical performance', and later when she thinks about Miss Arrowsmith:

that a girl whose appearance you could not characterise except by saying that her figure was slight and of middle stature, her features small, her eyes tolerable and her complexion sallow, had nevertheless a certain mental superiority which could not be explained away—an exasperating thorough-ness in her musical accomplishment, a fastidious discrimination in her general tastes, which made it impossible to force her admiration and kept you in awe of her standard. (36)

For all her poise, her cleverness, her appearance of easy mastery in nearly every situation, Gwendolen, we must by now realize, is not going to find life easy. She is capable of being kept in awe of standards she does not fully understand, and we have already seen that she is capable of terror and remorse. So far she has no outlet for such feelings: they have no place in the constricting repertoire of roles she chooses to play, and she cannot live out of a role except in outbursts of irritation. What she has yet to learn is, simply and spontaneously, to be herself; and the ease and skill of her performances are likely to make it very hard for her to abandon them.

It is not surprising, then, that Rex's proposal of marriage should frighten her in ways that she cannot fully understand. What Rex demands is an emotional response of some kind to his own feelings for her, and the demand is a threat to her artificial poise.

'Southampton! That's a stupid place to go to, isn't it?' said Gwendolen, chilly.

'It would be to me, because you would not be there.'

Silence.

'Should you mind about my going away, Gwendolen?'

'Of course. Every one is of consequence in this dreary country', said Gwendolen, curtly. The perception that poor Rex wanted to be tender made her curl up and harden like a sea-anemone at the touch of a finger. (58)

The implications of that image are at least partly physical, but what it points to is not an inherent frigidity in Gwendolen. Her aversion from Rex's tenderness indicates her terror at the incursion of forces that cannot be entirely controlled into the life that she is accustomed to command and treat as a series of diversions. 'The life of passion', George Eliot comments rather enigmatically, 'had begun negatively in her.' Gwendolen's response to Rex's tenderness—but not before he has left the house—is hysterical.

'I shall never love anybody. I can't love people. I hate them.'

'The time will come, dear, the time will come.'

Gwendolen was more and more convulsed with sobbing; but putting her arms round her mother's neck with an almost painful clinging, she said brokenly, 'I can't bear any one to be very near me but you.'

Then the mother began to sob, for this spoiled child had never shown such dependence on her before: so they clung to each other. (59)

George Eliot's comments on the people in her novels are exceptionally illuminating, but, as I have suggested in an earlier chapter, it is in her weakest novel that her commentaries remain more vividly in our memories than the narrated events. In *Daniel Deronda* it is always, I think, the events that we remember; the comments are more completely subordinated to them than in any of the earlier novels. It is as if the artist's sense of reality, her knowledge of how these imagined people really would react on each other, has achieved such sureness that she no longer has the same impulse to persuade the reader that people do in fact behave in such ways. She is still free to comment, and still does so, but her penetrating psychological insight is manifest in what she shows us happening: her comments only help us—and perhaps they helped George Eliot—to come to terms with the reality that she has shown us.

There are some aspects of Gwendolen that we are left to see for ourselves with very little help from the novelist as commentator. One of them is the nature of that revulsion from Rex's tenderness; perhaps we should need resources of language to describe it that were not available to George Eliot—the resources that D. H. Lawrence developed. George Eliot can only present, she cannot adequately explain, the difference between Gwendolen's hysterical revulsion from Rex's offer of love and her wholly healthy, potentially saving, revulsion from physical contact with Lush:

It was hardly a bow that Gwendolen gave—rather, it was the slightest forward sweep of the head away from the physiognomy that inclined itself towards her, and she immediately moved towards her seat, saying, 'I want to put on my burnous.' No sooner had she reached it, than Mr. Lush was there, and had the burnous in his hand: to annoy this supercilious young lady, he would incur the offence of forestalling Grandcourt; and, holding up the garment, close to Gwendolen, he said, 'Pray, permit me?' But she, wheeling away from him as if he had been a muddy hound, glided on to the ottoman, saying 'No, thank you.' (89)

This physical antipathy seems to me to be potentially saving because it is Gwendolen's instinctive revulsion from a real nastiness in the man (about whom we know more than she does at this stage)—and it shows that she *has* instinctive, physical responses that are fundamentally healthy. They do not, in fact, save her from marrying Grandcourt, partly because he has the skill, or the cleverness, to avoid presenting himself to Gwendolen in any but social terms: he does not make her aware of him as a lover.

When Gwendolen first meets Grandcourt, their conversation is described at length; a sample must suffice here as a reminder of the effect of the whole.

'I used to think archery was a great bore', Grandcourt began. He spoke with a fine accent, but with a certain broken drawl, as of a distinguished personage with a distinguished cold on his chest.

'Are you converted today?' said Gwendolen.

(Pause, during which she imagined various degrees and modes of opinion about herself that might be entertained by Grandcourt.)

'Yes, since I saw you shooting. In things of this sort one generally sees people missing and simpering.'

'I suppose you are a first-rate shot with a rifle.'

(Pause, during which Gwendolen, having taken a rapid observation of Grandcourt, made a brief graphic description of him to an indefinite hearer.)

'I have left off shooting.' (80)

Those pauses seem a little disconcerting at first, but they are finally reassuring to Gwendolen: clearly Grandcourt's habit is not to speak or act spontaneously. Everything he says is deliberate, even calculated; and however grim this may be as a warning of his invulnerability to spontaneous feeling, it is a guarantee for Gwendolen that he will not demand any expression of real feeling from her. In fact all Grandcourt's contributions to the conversation observe the conventions of a social game. Even when he says, 'Do you like danger?' he is not demanding a real response from her but providing her with a welcome opportunity to talk about herself and to present to him the image of herself that she chooses to cultivate. The conversation is a demanding one in terms of the social game, but utterly undemanding emotionally. Its opening topics are archery and boredom, and of these, boredom is the one that lasts, as the underlying theme of the whole encounter. Gwendolen has herself often affected boredom, and evidently regards as it as a well-bred and distinguished feeling.

So Grandcourt's manner flatters Gwendolen that she is secure in the social role she chooses to play, while we have ample evidence that although she plays it well she plays it precariously. The illusion of security is strengthened by those pauses— Gwendolen's mind frisking nimbly between Grandcourt's utterances has a sense of being far quicker than his, of running circles round him. In subsequent conversations, or matches, between them, Gwendolen's sense of playing skilfully and dominating the situation is more and more as if a fish should pride itself on the skill with which it plays the bait. Our awareness of her danger is what gives its breath-taking irony to Gwendolen's reflections about Grandcourt as a potential husband.

He did not appear to enjoy anything much. That was not necessary: and the less he had of particular tastes or desires, the more freedom his wife was likely to have in following hers. Gwendolen conceived that after marriage she would most probably be able to manage him thoroughly. (100)

The reader has by now the advantage of having seen Grand-court displayed in his home, where he is not impressing Gwendolen:

Fetch, the beautiful liver-coloured water-spaniel, which sat with its fore-paws firmly planted and its expressive brown face turned upward, watching Grandcourt with unshaken constancy. He held in his lap a tiny Maltese dog with a tiny silver collar and bell, and when he had a hand unused by cigar or coffee-cup, it rested on this small parcel of animal warmth. I fear that Fetch was jealous, and wounded that her master gave her no word or look; at last it seemed that she could bear this neglect no longer, and she gently put her large silky paw on her master's leg. Grandcourt looked at her with unchanged face for half a minute, and then took the trouble to lay down his cigar while he lifted the unimpassioned Fluff close to his chin and gave it caressing pats, all the while gravely watching Fetch, who, poor thing, whimpered inter-ruptedly, as if trying to repress that sign of discontent, and at last rested her head beside the appealing paw, looking up with piteous beseeching...But when the amusing anguish burst forth in a howling bark, Grandcourt pushed Fetch down without speaking, and, depositing Fluff carelessly on the table... began to look to his cigar, and found, with some annoyance against Fetch as the cause, that the brute of a cigar required relighting. Fetch, having begun to wail, found, like others of her sex, that it was not easy to leave off; indeed, the second howl was a louder one, and the third was like unto it.

'Turn out that brute, will you?' said Grandcourt to Lush, without raising his voice or looking at him—as if he counted on attention to the smallest sign. (90)

We are told shortly afterwards of Grandcourt's 'sense that he might kick Lush if he chose—only he never did choose to kick any animal, because...a gentleman's dogs should be kicked for him.' It is a memorable and witty comment, but we already know it from what we have seen and heard in the passage I have quoted: the later comment merely confirms it. It is not necessary —it seems even impossible—to understand Grandcourt, but we are made intensely aware of him. Common human experience, discovered by looking into our own hearts, can offer no account of Grandcourt, and a part of the significance of this passage is the suggestion that our experience of normal human feelings can enable us to conjecture the feelings of the dog more surely than those of Grandcourt. The nearest approach to 'Which of us has not...' or 'Have we not all...' in this passage is 'like others of her sex', which is about Fetch.

Grandcourt's mind is more inaccessible than a dog's: he is as incalculable as a lizard. The reptilian image occurs, and is developed, in Gwendolen's sense of him on page 100, and recurs from then on. At first, to Gwendolen, it suggests a strangeness and a fascination; later it becomes more explicitly repulsive. The image is an important one in respect of George Eliot's development as a novelist. The question that has always, in her earlier novels, been insistently pressing—how can a sympathetic understanding of a man's motives be pursued without weakening the bases of moral judgment?—becomes inapplicable if not utterly absurd in respect of a lizard. Celia in *Middlemarch* had seemed 'no more in need of salvation than a squirrel,' and Hetty in *Adam Bede* had evoked animal analogies, but it is only in *Daniel Deronda* that George Eliot offers us, as a consistently and fully imagined possibility, a man who must be regarded as utterly inaccessible to sympathetic understanding. If we could see his motives sympathetically—as George Eliot seems to insist we can, in *Middlemarch*, even with the most despicable people—it would not, with Grandcourt, be a morally enriching exercise in widening one's sympathies: it would be, in the end, moral suicide.

Gwendolen's acceptance of Grandcourt's proposal is prepared by the chapters in which she confronts what she takes to be economic realities, and is finally (it is a very different experience) confronted by them. From

'My life is my own affair. And I think'—here her tone took an edge of scorn —'I think I can do better for you than let you live in Sawyer's Cottage'

(174)

to

'Mamma, don't speak to me now. It is useless to cry and waste our strength over what can't be altered. You will live at Sawyer's Cottage, and I am going to the bishop's daughters. There is no more to be said...'   (197)

is a long step: long enough at any rate for marriage with Grand-court to seem a liberating prospect rather than a surrender of splendid possibilities of life. Herr Klesmer's frank advice has intervened—the cruel but necessary honesty of his opening Gwendolen's eyes to the folly of believing that she can be a singer or an actress as an easy way to wealth and fame. Herr Klesmer is one of the points of reference in the novel, representing a positive standard by which we see clearly what Gwendolen is not; as an artist he has the authority that can affirm, in response to her request for advice,

'You are a beautiful young lady—you have been brought up in ease—you have done what you would—you have not said to yourself, "I must know this exactly", "I must understand this exactly", "I must do this exactly"',—in uttering these three terrible *musts*, Klesmer lifted up three long fingers in succession. 'In sum, you have not been called upon to be anything but a charming young lady, whom it is an impoliteness to find fault with.'

(189)

His penetrating clarification of the difference between the dedi-cated artist and the accomplished young lady makes nonsense of Gwendolen's 'plan' to provide for herself and her mother and sisters. 'You would of course earn nothing—you could get no engagements for a long time', he observes in passing: he shows her that the life she has been proposing to herself as a means of escaping poverty is in fact an arduous vocation in which poverty is among the least of the hardships to be accepted.

Lizard or not, Grandcourt has a perfectly adequate under-standing of Gwendolen, and calculates his proposal accordingly. The previous chapter has vividly presented Gwendolen's appre-hension of the only alternative to marriage; George Eliot has led us to see that becoming a governess *is* a horrible fate for Gwendo-len, even though it need not be so for a different person—which is a consequence of the homage that the novel exacts for Gwendo-len from us. So we are with Gwendolen in feeling her choice to be a very difficult one, in which moral and material questions are finely balanced and intricately linked. Grandcourt's approach to the direct question compels Gwendolen to think of the conse-quences of her answer for her mother and sisters.

All the while they were looking at each other; and Grandcourt said, slowly and languidly, as if it were of no importance, other things having been settled—

'You will tell me now, I hope, that Mrs. Davilow's loss of fortune will not trouble you further. You will trust me to prevent it from weighing upon her. You will give me the claim to provide against that.'   (224)

His slow and languid manner is habitual, but could hardly have been more effective if it were calculated. For Gwendolen, it is a promise that no emotional demands are to be made of her. This implied assurance that he will not come near to her is contained in all he says and does, and more significantly in all he does not say and do, throughout the conversation, and it is essential to the success of his proposal. For at any moment, a fully *physical* sense of Grandcourt as a man—a man to hold and to be held by—could have given Gwendolen that shudder of spontaneous and sane revulsion that could have saved her (if going into service with the Momperts can be seen as salvation). Even after her acceptance of him, 'She had no alarm lest he meant to kiss her'; it is Grandcourt's 'style' that has succeeded in keeping even his proposal of marriage within the limits of a purely social relationship, keeping her at her ease in a social sense, avoiding any word or movement that could awaken her physical awareness of him.

In Grandcourt and Gwendolen, George Eliot for the first time gives us major characters fully realized from the outside. That, I think, is the most important point to be made about the difference between Gwendolen and George Eliot herself: not the fact that the novelist here portrays a girl who moves in County society, unlike herself, but that the texture of Gwendolen's being is radically different from her own. Gwendolen is in hardly any sense an extension of George Eliot herself, a construction upon her own character, or (what amounts to much the same) upon her notion of a universal human nature which the reader can be invited to confirm by introspection. I have suggested that for the novelist of *Middlemarch* the great key to character was 'Have we not all...?' or 'Which of us has not...?' In *Daniel Deronda* she has perfected another entry—to speak generally, that of Dickens and Conrad—the intense awareness that can transcend the need to understand.

This is what enables her in this novel to come nearer than ever before to doing justice to the varied complexity of human life—enables her to present qualities which are *not* held in common: the uniqueness, the utter unpredictability of each individual destiny, never repeated, whether it is near to or remote from the norms implied in 'general laws' governing human life.

The supremely abnormal destiny in the novel is, of course, Daniel Deronda's. He is to be a wholly admirable and extraordinary man, who deserves respect and even devotion, the quality of whose life is to reveal wider possibilities to Gwendolen. Rather as Herr Klesmer has exposed the smallness of her artistic talents by being, recognizably and commandingly, an artist, Deronda is to awaken in her a creative discontent with her constricted and immature moral being. It is by his standards, and, in the first chapter of the novel, through his eyes that we are invited to ponder Gwendolen's actual and potential moral force.

> Was she beautiful or not beautiful? and what was the secret of form or expression which gave the dynamic quality to her glance? Was the good or the evil genius dominant in those beams? Probably the evil; else why was the effect that of unrest rather than of undisturbed charm? Why was the wish to look again felt as coercion and not as a longing in which the whole being consents? (1)

Looking at Gwendolen is here shown as a complex pleasure, not at all a simple aesthetic delight but a morally strenuous activity. The opening of the novel seems to promise further investigation of such complexities in a man's looking at a fascinating woman—an investigation that might be expected to enrich one's awareness of the subtle interactions of goodness and beauty. And one expects Deronda's to be the eye that will show us the nature of a whole response to Gwendolen.

In some respects this promise is fulfilled. Deronda is, it seems, qualified to attain, if anybody can, the whole vision of Gwendolen. The nature of his qualification can perhaps be suggested by comparison with Klesmer, who *can* take a simple delight in looking at her, even while she sings, as long as she makes no claim to be an artist. Once she presents herself to him in *that* light, as we have seen, Klesmer judges her pretensions ruthlessly; but this only happens briefly. A moral being, however, she must be all her life, whether she likes it or not, merely because she is human; and it is as a moral being that she appeals to Deronda's judgment. Her uneasy sense of being judged by standards that she has not encountered elsewhere leads her to ask him why he thinks it wrong for her to gamble; it is the beginning of her moral education.

Here, as elsewhere in the novel, Gwendolen turns to Deronda as to the only person she knows whom she can talk to about her deepest anxieties. He is interested in what she is, not in the quality of her performance, social or artistic; he does not deflect conversation on to a merely social level when she asks him a serious question. From their first encounter he is interested in her; as he becomes necessary to her, he responds to her need with a deepening concern for her; but he is not in love with her. All these things contribute to make him an important, and increasingly important, part of her life. To these we must add a certain air of authority that commands Gwendolen's respect; and it is hard to see how Gwendolen's development through the novel could be imagined to take place without such a man.

Unfortunately he is far less convincing to us in his own person than in his influence on Gwendolen's life. Consider this piece of conversation, remembering that Deronda is a man—a very unusual one, but a man—talking to a woman not much younger than himself. Gwendolen says:

'You admire Miss Lapidoth because you think her blameless, perfect. And you know you would despise a woman who had done something you thought very wrong.'

'That would depend entirely on her own view of what she had done', said Deronda.

'You would be satisfied if she were very wretched, I suppose?' said Gwendolen, impetuously.

'No, not satisfied—full of sorrow for her...I did not mean to say that the finer nature is not more adorable; I meant that those who would be comparatively uninteresting beforehand may become worthier of sympathy when they do something that awakens in them a keen remorse. Lives are enlarged in different ways. I daresay some would never get their eyes opened if it were not for a violent shock from the consequences of their own actions. And

when they are suffering in that way one must care for them more than for
the comfortably self-satisfied.' Deronda forgot everything but his vision of
what Gwendolen's experience had probably been, and urged by compassion
let his eyes and voice express as much interest as they would.   (330)

It is not easy to explain, if it needs explaining, why one feels that
a man could not speak to Gwendolen quite like that. A woman,
much older than Gwendolen, perhaps could: perhaps this is a
way of expressing a suspicion that George Eliot herself is speaking
here—using Deronda's voice to say what *she* would have liked to
say to Gwendolen. Coming from a man, the curiously generalizing
speech contrives to be, at the same time, offensively distant and
embarrassingly intimate. (No doubt the novelist intended it to be
finely balanced between the two.) Another way of putting it
might be to say that a man could not decently adopt that tone in
speaking to a woman unless he meant to marry her.

It can hardly be denied, in fact, especially in their later conversations, that Deronda's advising makes Gwendolen dependent
on him to an extent that George Eliot shows no sign of realizing;
if he *had* meant to gain power over her, he could hardly have set
about it more effectively. But when Sir Hugo warns Deronda not
to 'flirt with her too much', it is clear that the novelist intends us
to share Deronda's exasperation at this 'tasteless joke'.

'I don't think you ever saw me flirt', said Deronda, not amused.
  'Oh, haven't I, though?' said Sir Hugo, provokingly. 'You are always
looking tenderly at the women, and talking to them in a Jesuitical way. You
are a dangerous young fellow—a king of Lovelace who will make the Clarissas
run after you instead of your running after them.'   (269)

It is as well—George Eliot implies—that Deronda should be
made explicitly aware of the ridiculous misconstruction that is
likely to be placed (by people of ordinarily limited imagination)
on his entirely disinterested concern for Gwendolen. We are not
encouraged to consider the possibility that there may be some
truth in the view. If Deronda had been more securely created,
she could have allowed this possibility to take its place within the
complexity of his motives; but he is only in part an artistic
creation—the rest of him is make-believe. So when Deronda is
briefly exposed to ridicule, he must be protected; when Grand-

court says, 'Do you take off your hat to the horses?' the author adds, 'said Grandcourt, with a slight sneer'—as if to forbid us to enjoy it.

In order to have the moral authority that can challenge Gwendolen's superficial complacency, Deronda must himself be capable of dedicating himself entirely to a worthy cause. This requirement does not, of course, completely account for the role of Zionism in the novel. It could have been satisfied by his dedication to any of a variety of causes; whereas, in the novel, Zionism is evidently not merely a suggestive example of a noble aim that might command a man's devotion, but becomes a major theme in its own right. It seems to me, though, that it is effectually present in the novel only to the extent I have suggested— as the cause to which Deronda dedicates himself—and that George Eliot does not succeed in making Zionism a live issue for the reader.

This is the most difficult critical problem that the novel presents. If we are inclined to say that this large part of the book is a failure, we must be careful to ensure that we are really responding from the heart, and not merely expressing a version of the commonplace scepticism of our time. We have to be on our guard against the prevalent eccentricity of the age we live in: our predisposition to disbelieve in the validity of any great cause, any aim beyond the limitations of our own lives, that could give a meaning to the lives of those who devoted themselves to it. So many heroic aspirations—social, political and intellectual—have in the last hundred years been fulfilled at enormous cost of self-sacrifice and suffering, and have begun to turn sour as soon as they were achieved; so much blood has been shed to save humanity, and we see humanity, to all appearances, no more saved than it ever was; so many heroes have laid down their lives, as the saying goes, to so little purpose as far as the enrichment of life is concerned—that we have reason to decline any invitation to heroic action, to question the motives of heroes, and to doubt whether any vast enterprise can really be taken seriously by a sane man.

All this is, as I suggested, part of the general eccentricity of the age we live in, and few of us are likely to be exempt from it. But in attempting to judge a work of art from a centrally human standpoint, we can at least remind ourselves that good causes exist, and can at least give a sense of direction (which we have no right to call illusory) to the lives of those actively engaged in them, whether they succeed or not. And although none of the heroic enterprises of the past has unquestionably 'saved' humanity, or civilization, or even a nation, once and for all, it is possible that they expressed an impulse without which we could not have survived as human beings.

This digression is necessary before I can plausibly assert that, whatever the mid-twentieth century thinks, heroic causes exist, and that we should not be prejudiced against Deronda's commitment to Zionism. Such a commitment, however, is perhaps the hardest thing for a novelist to create—especially such a novelist as George Eliot, whose finest insights have generally been into the common lot of humanity and the need to accept its limitations in order to grow up. Recognizing the goodness of a cause is a matter of belief—which, as D. H. Lawrence says in his brilliant essay 'A Propos of *Lady Chatterley's Lover*', is 'a profound emotion that has the mind's connivance'. It cannot be merely a matter of intellectual conviction: this can only justify adherence to the cause—it cannot itself provide the impetus. My experience, which is here shared with many others, is that George Eliot has failed to convey the passionate impulse of Zionism in Deronda's life, however skilfully she procures the mind's connivance. She answers every possible objection to Deronda's dedication to the cause, but does not make us feel its positive necessity, its emotional reality. The emotion in that part of the novel is the earnestness of her wish to make it true.

We have to respond somehow to her strenuous attempt. Here she describes Deronda's visit to a synagogue in Germany, and is clearly trying to evoke the texture of the experience as she did in *Silas Marner* with Silas's recollections of the Lantern Yard.

The Hebrew liturgy, like others, has its transitions of litany, lyric, proclamation, dry statement and blessing; but this evening all were one for Deronda: the chant of the *Chazan's* or Reader's grand wide-ranging voice with its passage from monotony to sudden cries, the outburst of sweet boys' voices from the little quire, the devotional swaying of men's bodies backwards and forwards, the very commonness of the building and shabbiness of the scene where a national faith, which had penetrated the thinking of half the world, and moulded the splendid forms of that world's religion, was finding a remote, obscure echo—all were blent for him as one expression of a binding history, tragic and yet glorious. (274)

What obstructs the presentation of Deronda's experience here is George Eliot's oppressive consciousness of the need to explain to her readers what he is responding to. As in many other parts of the novel, she is erudite and informative: she has undertaken an educational task. However thoroughly she performs it, this activity is different from—and less than—the novelist's art. One expects to be educated by a novel, but this is not the kind of education for which the novel is the proper medium. And even in a travel-book we should resist, I think, the intrusive didacticism —or display—of 'the *Chazan*'s or Reader's...' In the same paragraph we have already had 'the *talith* or white blue-fringed kind of blanket' and 'the *almenor* or platform'—none of which is strictly necessary to the novel.

This is not to suggest that 'the Jewish part' of the novel should be neglected. Much of it consists of imagined incidents fully realized, and the Cohen family is as finely achieved as the Meyricks. And even Mordecai, whose speeches often strike us as tedious, is in some respects an artistic triumph:

'I cherish nothing for the Jewish nation, I seek nothing for them, but the good which promises good to all the nations. The spirit of our religious life, which is one with our national life, is not hatred of aught but wrong. The Masters have said, an offence against man is worse than an offence against God. But what wonder if there is hatred in the breasts of Jews, who are children of the ignorant and oppressed—what wonder, since there is hatred in the breasts of Christians? Our national life was a growing light. Let the central fire be kindled again, and the light will reach afar.' (404)

This is only a sample of Mordecai's language; its full effect depends on its momentum—even, sometimes, its tedium. George Eliot has created, in the mouth of Mordecai, an example of the rhetoric of the visionary. Its texture can be compared with that of revolutionary visionaries today: not practical reformers, or politicians with clearly definable policies, but those who demand first that we embrace the vision, and brush aside our cautions about immediate tactics and practical consequences. Embrace the vision, they insist; be wholehearted for *such* a future; then your tactics will be made clear by the opportunities that appear. To discuss practical difficulties before embracing the vision is merely to make excuses for inertia.

Mordecai is undeniably, even insistently, a fact in the novel. Deronda has to make a decision which cannot be entirely rational —whether he will regard Mordecai as a prophet or a madman. There is no possible compromise. After the long speech from which my quotation is taken,

Every one felt that the talk was ended, and the tone of phlegmatic discussion made unseasonable by Mordecai's high-pitched solemnity. It was as if they had come together to hear the blowing of the *shophar*, and had nothing to do now but to disperse. (405)

The analogy suggests very clearly the quality of Mordecai's rhetoric; there is no possible moderate and reasonable response, so discussion would be inappropriate. Whatever the faults—of over-insistence and didacticism—in the presentation of Mordecai, his voice is made distinctive enough to give the reader a vivid sense of Deronda's dilemma, which is described at the beginning of Book VI (aptly called *Revelations*).

Deronda's decision is made partly as a result of a series of coincidences or miracles. No law of nature is suspended, but sequences of events occur that seem to point in one direction. Like so much of the Zionist theme, they are negatively credible— we can find no grounds for denying their possibility, but they do not present themselves to us as recognizable examples of the way life is. George Eliot is trying with some success to extend the range of her fiction beyond the analysis of the common human lot and the general laws, more or less fixed, that govern it, to include in the scope of her art those moments of strangeness that are characteristic of life and fact. But the success is limited to the single incident; the accumulation fails to convince.

Is it the strangeness, the unaverage quality of her own destiny that George Eliot is trying to match, or approach, in her last novel? The only limitation of the world she portrays in her earlier novels is that it could not accommodate her own life. In *Daniel Deronda* she seems to be making a deliberate attempt, which does not entirely succeed, to see clearly and wholly a world that is recognizably governed by the same familiar laws as that of *Middlemarch*, but where at the same time, as in reality, uncommon people can find or make their strange and rare destinies, under the influence of events that can sometimes seem not to be entirely accidental. Perhaps that is why we find, in the parts that fail, so much evidence of how desperately hard she tried: the final challenge of her art was to create an imagined reality comparable in fullness with the reality she had herself experienced.

But we should not pursue too far such speculations about the relation between the art and the artist's life. *Daniel Deronda* is (with *Silas Marner*) the least autobiographical of the novels, and our reading of it does not need to be sustained by such extraneous interests or puzzles. In this account I have dwelt on the expressive force of incidents presented without commentary; but I propose to end with a quotation that will serve as an example of George Eliot's comments at their finest. Lydia Glasher has just been told by Grandcourt that he intends to marry Gwendolen, and the imagery with which her reaction is described is at the same time fully responsive and analytically detached, fantasmagoric and lucid.

'You didn't always see the necessity.'

'Perhaps not. I see it now.'

In those few undertoned words of Grandcourt's she felt as absolute a resistance as if her thin fingers had been pushing at a fast-shut iron door. She knew her helplessness, and shrank from testing it by any appeal—shrank from crying in a dead ear and clinging to dead knees, only to see the immovable face and feel the rigid limbs. She did not weep nor speak: she was too hard pressed by the sudden certainty which has as much of chill sickness in it as of thought and emotion. The defeated clutch of struggling hope gave her in these first moments a horrible sensation. At last she rose with a spasmodic effort, and, unconscious of everything but her wretchedness, pressed her forehead against the hard cold glass of the window. The children, playing on the gravel, took this as a sign that she wanted them, and running forward stood in front of her with their sweet faces upturned expectantly. This roused her: she shook her head at them, waved them off and overcome with this painful exertion sank back in the nearest chair.